M000086934

BUILT-INS
CABINETS
& SHELVES

Editors of *Fine Homebuilding* & *Fine Woodworking*

The Taunton Press

© 2018 by The Taunton Press, Inc.
All rights reserved.

THE TAUNTON PRESS, INC.
63 South Main Street
Newtown, CT 06470-2344
e-mail: tp@taunton.com

EDITORS: Peter Chapman, Christina Glennon
COPY EDITOR: Seth Reichgott
INDEXER: Jay Kreider
JACKET/COVER DESIGN: Teresa Fernandes
INTERIOR DESIGN: carol singer | notice design
LAYOUT: Rita Sowins / Sowins Design
COVER PHOTOGRAPHERS: Dillon Ryan (front cover and back cover, left photo); Michael Pekovich (back cover, right photo)

The following names/manufacturers appearing in *Built-Ins, Shelves, & Cabinets* are trademarks: Accuride®, Aristokraft®, Benjamin Moore®, Bertch®, Bressmeyer®, Blum®, Brusso®, Canyon Creek®, Ceramithane®, Cheerios®, Chemetal®, Decora®, Delta®, Festool®, Graco®, Grass®, Häfele®, Homecrest®, Kemper®, Knape & Vogt®, KraftMaid®, Masonite®, MasterBrand®, Merillat®, Omega®, Polyx®, Rev-A-Shelf®, Saint-Astier®, Schrock®, Sherwin-Williams®, SketchUp®, UL®

Library of Congress Cataloging-in-Publication Data

Title: Built-ins, shelves & cabinets / editors of Fine Homebuilding & Fine
  Woodworking.
Other titles: Built-ins, shelves and cabinets | Fine homebuilding. | Fine
  woodworking.
Description: Newtown, CT : The Taunton Press, Inc., 2018. | Includes index.
Identifiers: LCCN 2017037052 | ISBN 9781631869129 (print) | ISBN 9781631869860 (pdf format) |
ISBN 9781631869884 (mobi format)
Subjects: LCSH: Built-in furniture. | Shelving (Furniture) | Storage cabinets.
Classification: LCC TT197.5.B8 .B855 2018 | DDC 684.16--dc23
LC record available at https://lccn.loc.gov/2017037052

Printed in the United States of America
10 9 8 7 6 5 4 3 2

ABOUT YOUR SAFETY: Working wood is inherently dangerous. Using hand or power tools improperly or ignoring safety practices can lead to permanent injury or even death. Don't try to perform operations you learn about here (or elsewhere) unless you're certain they are safe for you. If something about an operation doesn't feel right, don't do it. Look for another way. We want you to enjoy the craft, so please keep safety foremost in your mind whenever you're in the shop.

ACKNOWLEDGMENTS

Special thanks to the authors, editors, art directors, copy editors, and other staff members of *Fine Woodworking* and *Fine Homebuilding* who contributed to the development of the chapters in this book.

Contents

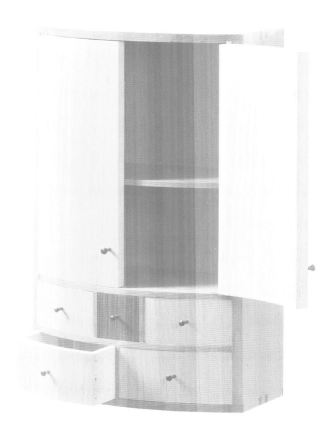

PART FOUR

Shelves and Bookcases

Introduction

From the plainest bookshelf to the most tricked-out built-in, every storage piece you build involves a blend of techniques, strategies, and style. This book, brimming with expert information from the pages of *Fine Homebuilding* and *Fine Woodworking* magazines, delivers a bounty of advice and inspiration in all three areas from today's premier craftsmen.

After laying the groundwork with sections on the safe use of the tablesaw and on selecting and using solid wood and plywood, the book presents projects that incorporate joinery techniques ranging from nails to dovetails and pocket screws to plunge-cut Domino tenons. It covers construction strategies that span the spectrum of on-site carpentry as well as in-shop cabinetmaking, turning a spotlight on everything from installing pre-made cabinets to site-building complex pieces suited for a unique space; and from screwing together a custom vanity to fashioning a frame-and-panel wall cabinet with coopered doors and hand-dovetailed drawers. The collection of projects is equally inclusive when it comes to style, presenting pieces inspired by everything from Shaker tables and Japanese tansu cabinets to Colonial country furniture and sleek urban contemporary work.

Running through all these diverse projects is a high level of craftsmanship and a shared obsession with function and practicality. Each of the pieces is an elegant answer to a set of real-world problems. But different houses present different challenges, so we've also included design advice that's more broadly applicable: how to plan a dining nook, for example; what height and angles are best for a built-in seat; how thick should shelves be to prevent sagging; and what considerations are most critical for the layout of a kitchen. If you've got some storage pieces to design and build, you've found the right book.

—Jonathan Binzen
Deputy Editor, *Fine Woodworking*

BASICS

Plywood for Woodworkers

TONY O'MALLEY

In my business making custom built-in cabinetry, I use more plywood and other sheet goods than solid wood. Whether I'm building kitchen cabinets, TV enclosures, window seats, or library shelves, manufactured panels of one type or another make up the lion's share of a project.

The secret to working with sheet goods is to master the balancing act of looks, strength, and cost when buying the material. Buying the best-looking plywood for every piece of a project can be an expensive proposition, particularly when less pricey sheet goods will work just as well, or even better, for painted cabinetry, drawer bottoms, shop furniture, or woodworking jigs.

Sheet goods have a lot of advantages over solid wood for certain projects. When making large or wide surfaces, sheet goods cost less, are stronger and more stable, and resist warping better than solid wood. They're also time-savers, since they needn't be jointed or planed.

There are dozens of varieties out there, but just four types will cover your needs. The first is furniture-grade plywood, which is distinguished by its high-quality face veneers. But you pay a premium for that quality, so this material should be saved for surfaces that will be displayed prominently. Cabinet-grade plywood, which has surface defects like knots, pins, and mineral stains, is cheaper than furniture-grade plywood, and is ideal for painted or hidden surfaces. Then there's multi-ply

Surface perfection. Using a furniture-grade cherry plywood for this built-in gives a fine furniture look without the warping and instability of solid wood. Plus, it's less expensive and easier to work with.

The Fab Four

Whether you're building kitchen cabinets, drawer parts, templates, or workshop jigs, these four go-to sheet goods can handle a huge variety of woodworking tasks and get you through a project more quickly and, in most cases, less expensively than solid wood. Learn to make the best choice by weighing the strengths, weaknesses, cost, and availability of each one.

FURNITURE-GRADE PLYWOOD

CABINET-GRADE PLYWOOD

MULTIPLY

MDF

plywood, usually Baltic birch, which is suitable for drawer boxes, jigs, and other shop tasks. Last is medium-density fiberboard (MDF), a sheet good made of fine wood particles compressed and glued together. It is a remarkably flat and inexpensive material well-suited for jigs, shop furniture, and as a substrate for veneering and countertop laminate.

Learning the different ways each is used—along with some lumberyard lingo—will help you pick the best panel for your project.

Furniture-grade is best in show

Pick furniture-grade plywood for large, conspicuous wood surfaces, and then choose a core suitable for how the panel will be used. For open casework, such as a bookcase or fireplace cabinetry, select veneer-core plywood with an A1 or A2 grade (see "Buyer's Guide to Furniture-Grade Plywood," p. 8). Veneer-core is the lightest of the plywoods and holds screws best, making construction much easier. Because it is light, it is less likely to sag when used for shelving or other long spans. Plus, it's easier to reinforce its edge by screwing it to a cabinet case or other support. In most cases, go with ¾-in. thickness.

On desktops and similar surfaces where flatness is critical, ¾-in. MDF-core panels are a better choice. They also tend to have better veneers and fewer flaws. In ½-in. and ¼-in. thicknesses, MDF-core is the best choice for cabinet doors or other framed panels, since its ultra-flat surface will look better when finished. Combination-core plywood works well in any of those situations, too. It combines the best of both worlds—the flatness of MDF and the holding power of plywood—and is an excellent all-around choice.

The best bet for purchasing furniture-grade panels is a retail lumberyard. Wholesale plywood dealers will sometimes sell to non-professional builders, usually on a cash-and-carry basis. Choosing between the three cores often depends on availability. As a rule of thumb, opt for the most flattering veneers available on a core that makes sense for the project at hand.

Cabinets, too. Use cabinet-grade plywood for painted cabinetry, such as these kitchen cabinets. Buying it prefinished with a clear coat is great for interiors, saving time and adding minimal expense.

Shop furniture. Cabinet-grade, veneer-core plywood holds screws well and is inexpensive, making it an excellent choice for shop furniture like this planer cart.

Cabinet-grades work behind the scenes

For painted or hidden surfaces, such as the backs and sides of cabinetry or drawer parts, go with cabinet-grade plywood. There's no need to spend extra money on faces that no one sees. Plus, it's widely available at both home centers and lumberyards and costs significantly less than furniture-grade panels.

Cabinet-grade plywood is almost always veneer-core and has rotary-sawn or plain-sliced veneers. For most of my projects, I use B-grade maple with plain-sliced veneers. I also make

Buyers' Guide to Furniture-Grade Plywood

Core considerations

For cabinetry and built-ins, I typically buy three different core types of furniture-grade plywood: veneer, MDF, and a combination of the two. **Veneer-core panels are the** most common, lightest, and usually the most **expensive. They can be fas**tened easily, but any flaws in their cores can **telegraph to the face vene**er, showing up after they're finished. MDF-core **panels have a smooth, eas**ily finished surface but are very heavy and don't **hold fasteners as well. Com**bination-core panels are a hybrid. Their inner **cores are made of hardwoo**d plies, sandwiched between layers of MDF. **They combine the strength** and screw-holding properties of a veneer core **with the surface perfection** of an MDF core.

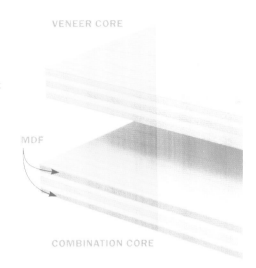

VENEER CORE

MDF

COMBINATION CORE

Making the grade

Grades for face veneers on domestic plywood use a letter-number combi**nation. The better face rec**eives a letter grade (AA, A, B, C, D, E) with AA **being the best, and the op**posite face receives a numerical grade of **1 through 4, with 1 being t**he best. Furniture-grade plywood is an AA or **A grade. I most often use A**-1 or A-2 panels, which have excellent-looking **face veneer on the front, an**d a veneer that is very close in appearance on **the back. For cabinet-grade** plywoods, I usually use a B-1, although home **centers often sell C grades** as cabinet-grade stock.

Two Ways to Slice Veneer

Plywood veneers are commonly cut from logs in **two ways. Rotary-cut venee**r is peeled like a paper **towel from its roll, producin**g a seamless, single **piece face. It's economical** but more bland-looking, **making it better suited for c**abinet-grade applica**tions. Plain-sliced veneer is** cut across the width of **a log just the way lumber is**. Usually it is random**matched, which can be mor**e natural-looking. It **also can be book-matched,** which produces mirror**image grain patterns. If you** need several panels **and are planning to use a cl**ear finish, ask for **sequential panels, which wi**ll have similar color **and grain characteristics.**

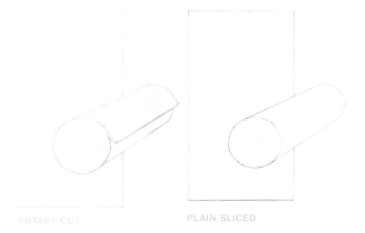

ROTARY-CUT

PLAIN-SLICED

drawer parts of cabinet-grade plywood, and use solid-wood edging to cover the cores.

Cabinet-grade plywood can be used for jigs and other woodworking accessories and fixtures. It is a bit pricier and less flat than MDF, but it holds screws better. Home centers sometimes sell cabinet-grade plywood, commonly with red oak, maple, or birch veneers.

Multi-ply fills many roles

Multi-ply plywoods are manufactured from thinner plies than normal veneer-core plywoods. They are pricier, but have cores that are virtually void-free and surfaces that are flatter than regular veneer-core plywood. They are also the only plywoods attractive enough to be used without edge-banding.

Distinctive drawers. Multi-ply is a good choice for drawer parts, as its void-free edges are attractive as is.

Multi-ply is a good choice for drawer parts, and its flatness and screw retention make it the best choice for jigs and shop furniture, too.

Baltic birch is the most common version, but Finnish birch, Russian birch, Appleply, Europly, and similar plywoods are also available. It's rotary-cut, and graded differently than standard plywood. Baltic birch, for instance, has both sides graded—from B, to BB, CP, and C, with B being the highest. Multi-ply is usually available through lumber dealers only.

MDF is a shop workhorse

MDF is a versatile, widely available sheet good that will work for a variety of furniture projects and woodshop tasks. Price is its main advantage.

MDF's stable, smooth faces make it an excellent material for cabinetry, door panels, and other projects that will have colored lacquers or paints. Plus, the edges can be shaped with a router bit, sanded smooth, and painted. Its ultra-flat surface makes it an excellent material for laminating with veneers or countertop material, or building jigs and workshop templates—particularly if they're curved.

There are a few downsides. At around 90 lb. per sheet, MDF is heavy, although some dealers sell "lightweight" versions that can reduce the weight by up to 30%. It does not hold screws well, although specialty fasteners such as T-nuts or Confirmat screws can help when joining pieces. Cutting MDF produces a lot of fine dust, so dust collection is a good idea. Water is a problem, too: It will cause MDF to swell and lose its structural integrity, so avoid uses where it will get wet, such as countertops or toe-kicks in a kitchen.

Flat panels. For painted, flat-panel doors, MDF will resist warping better than plywood. Glue it into the grooves for added stability.

Top choice for templates. When building tenoning jigs and other jigs, MDF's flatness and cost make it an excellent choice. It's easily shaped too, making it a good choice for templates.

The Language of the Lumberyard

STEVE SCOTT

Buying wood at a lumberyard is like ordering dinner in a French restaurant. For the unprepared, the choices are confusing, the menu offers scant help, and the waiter speaks a foreign language. Asking for what you want can be an intimidating and frustrating experience. On the other hand, the offerings in a French restaurant are richer and more varied than the average fast-food joint. Master a few key phrases, and you can eat like a king.

For the woodworker who usually buys stock from the home center, the lumberyard or hardwood retailer offers a similar step up in quality and variety. It gives you the chance to buy roughsawn stock and mill it to dimension yourself, freeing you creatively from the standard thicknesses of pre-surfaced material. Study the dialect of the lumberyard and you'll soon be making sense of the wide variety available there, choosing wisely and dealing confidently with the host (the person driving the forklift).

What follows is a kind of English-to-lumberyard phrase book. Study it and take it with you on your next trip to buy wood.

How it's measured: When an inch isn't an inch

Lumberyards measure a roughsawn board's thickness in ¼-in. increments, so 4/4 (four-quarter) stock is 1 in. thick, 8/4 stock is 2 in. thick, and so on. If your project calls for finished pieces 1 in. thick, you'll want to buy

ROUGHSAWN: Planks that haven't been squared or smoothed and are still hatch-marked by the large blades at the sawmill.

S4S: Surfaced on four sides. Both faces are planed smooth and both edges ripped straight.

SKIP-PLANED: A board that has been partially planed on one side to reveal some of the wood's grain and color underneath the roughsawn mill marks. Also called hit-and-miss planing.

How It's Measured

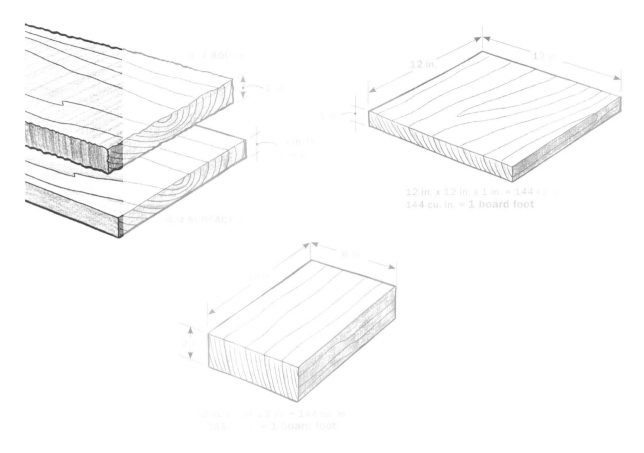

12 in. x 12 in. x 1 in. = 144 cu. in.
144 cu. in. = 1 board foot

5/4 roughsawn stock to allow for losses as you mill them smooth. When you buy boards that have already been surfaced, the stated thickness will match the board's original roughsawn thickness. The actual thickness will typically be $^3/_{16}$ in. to $^1/_4$ in. less.

When a foot isn't a foot

Lumberyard operators say one of the biggest challenges new customers face is in understanding the board foot—the basic unit of measurement for roughsawn stock. The board foot (144 cubic in.) is confusing because it measures a board's volume, not its length. This means that a piece of stock 1 ft.

long can contain more than 1 board foot of material. A good visual way to understand 1 board foot is to picture a board 1 in. thick by 12 in. wide and 12 in long. Add an inch to the board's thickness, and you now have 2 board feet. To calculate a plank's board footage, multiply its thickness by its length and width (all in inches) and divide the result by 144.

In contrast, surfaced lumber is typically sold by the linear foot, a simple measurement of a board's length. The price per foot will vary according to the board's width and thickness.

One Board, Many Woods

A single log contains different types of wood, with very different properties and appearance, depending on how it is cut.

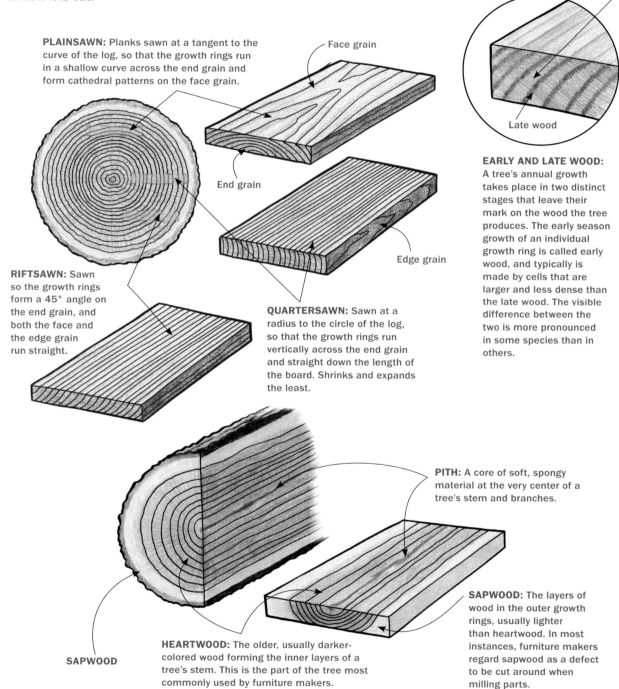

PLAINSAWN: Planks sawn at a tangent to the curve of the log, so that the growth rings run in a shallow curve across the end grain and form cathedral patterns on the face grain.

Face grain

End grain

Edge grain

Early wood

Late wood

EARLY AND LATE WOOD: A tree's annual growth takes place in two distinct stages that leave their mark on the wood the tree produces. The early season growth of an individual growth ring is called early wood, and typically is made by cells that are larger and less dense than the late wood. The visible difference between the two is more pronounced in some species than in others.

RIFTSAWN: Sawn so the growth rings form a 45° angle on the end grain, and both the face and the edge grain run straight.

QUARTERSAWN: Sawn at a radius to the circle of the log, so that the growth rings run vertically across the end grain and straight down the length of the board. Shrinks and expands the least.

PITH: A core of soft, spongy material at the very center of a tree's stem and branches.

SAPWOOD: The layers of wood in the outer growth rings, usually lighter than heartwood. In most instances, furniture makers regard sapwood as a defect to be cut around when milling parts.

SAPWOOD

HEARTWOOD: The older, usually darker-colored wood forming the inner layers of a tree's stem. This is the part of the tree most commonly used by furniture makers.

Hardwood Lumber Grades

FAS (First and Second)

Boards must be at least 6 in. wide and 8 ft. long, and each must yield clear pieces totaling 83% of the board's face. The clear pieces must be at least 3 in. wide by 7 ft. or 4 in. wide by 5 ft. Both faces of the board must meet these requirements to be graded FAS.

F1F (FAS One Face)

A step down from FAS, in which the board's better face must meet all the FAS requirements and the opposite face must meet the standards for No. 1 Common.

Selects

Essentially the same as F1F except that the minimum overall board size is reduced to 4 in. wide and 6 ft. long.

No. 1 Common

Sometimes called cabinet grade. Boards must be at least 3 in. wide and 4 ft. long, with clear pieces totaling between 66% and 83% of the board's face. The clear boards must be at least 3 in. wide by 3 ft. long or 4 in. wide by 2 ft. long. Both faces must meet these requirements to be graded No. 1 Common.

No. 2A Common

Sometimes called economy grade. Overall size requirements are the same as for No. 1 Common, but the clear cuttings need only total 50% of the original face. If either face of a board is graded as No. 2A, then the board's grade is 2A, regardless of the opposite face.

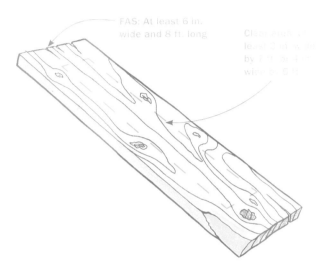

FAS: At least 6 in. wide and 8 ft. long

Clear piece at least 3 in. wide by 7 ft. or 4 in. wide by 5 ft.

Hardwood lumber grades

Established by the National Hardwood Lumber Association, these grades are based on the percentage of clear wood, or wood that is free from certain defects like checks, knots, pitch pockets, and sticker stain (see "What to Look Out For" on the facing page). The upper grades yield clear pieces that are longer and wider than those from the lower grades. Naturally, they also cost more. It's not crucial to memorize all the rules, but it helps to know which grades yield larger, clear boards versus smaller ones. Knowing the lumber grades can help you figure out which pile to sort through, whether you need smaller stock for, say, a wall-hung cabinet, or larger, clear boards for a dining table.

What to Look Out For

One of the best ways to ensure flat, square stock is to leave bad boards at the lumberyard. But a little perspective is important, because, nature being what it is, every board is imperfect in some way. So, when you're sorting through the stacks, bear in mind that many defects can be milled away or cut around. For example, a badly bowed long board can be cut into smaller lengths to make the problem manageable.

CHECKS: A separation of the end-grain fibers or a lengthwise opening on a board's face (surface checking). Caused by shrinkage due to rapid drying. Considered a defect for grading purposes.

KNOT: Cross-section of a branch that intersects the main stem and appears in a sawn plank. A sound knot is solid across its face and as hard as the surrounding wood. Knots are considered defects for grading purposes.

PIN-KNOT: A sound knot with a diameter not more than ¼ in.

STICKER STAIN: A mark left on the board from a sticker, a board inserted between layers of stacked lumber for air circulation. If the stain can't be removed by milling, it's considered a defect.

WANE: Bark or the lack of wood at a board's edge caused by the round edge of the log. A defect for grading purposes.

Every Warp Has a Name

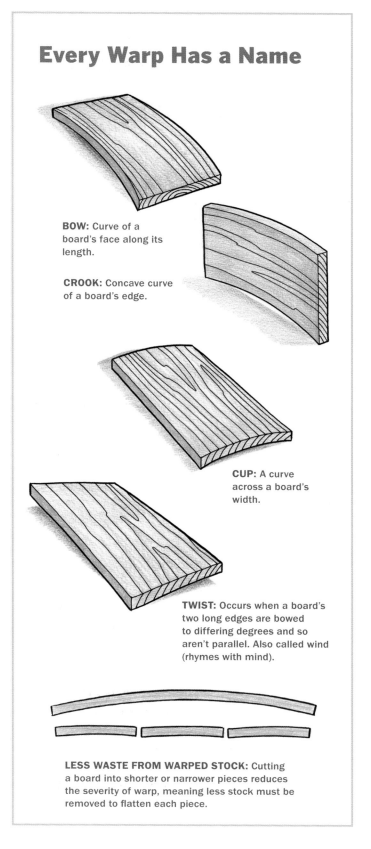

BOW: Curve of a board's face along its length.

CROOK: Concave curve of a board's edge.

CUP: A curve across a board's width.

TWIST: Occurs when a board's two long edges are bowed to differing degrees and so aren't parallel. Also called wind (rhymes with mind).

LESS WASTE FROM WARPED STOCK: Cutting a board into shorter or narrower pieces reduces the severity of warp, meaning less stock must be removed to flatten each piece.

Staying Safe on the Tablesaw

Most woodworkers, including me, will answer yes to the following two questions, while looking sheepishly at their penny loafers. Did you ignore the "Using Your Saw" section in the owner's manual when you got your first tablesaw? Have you experienced kickback?

I have had workpieces kick back a few times in my life. Fortunately, I wasn't hurt. For others, though, that instant on the tablesaw has been tragic and life-altering.

With hundreds of students passing through my school each year, I've developed firm guidelines for safe tablesaw use, regardless of skill level. My first rule is to keep all 13 saws properly set up and maintained. But this article focuses on the second part of the equation: a knowledgeable operator. If you understand how the saw works and know the best practices for its use, the chance for a bad accident can be virtually eliminated. Machines don't think, but you can.

Kickback is the main danger

Kickback accounts for the majority of tablesaw accidents. Unfortunately, I encounter many woodworkers who don't understand the cause of kickback, or the cure.

Here's how it happens. The teeth at the front of the blade do the cutting, and they move downward, helping to keep the board safely on the table. But the teeth at the back of the blade are not your friend; they spin in your direction at over 100 mph. During a safe cut, the slot made by the blade brushes past the back teeth without incident. But if the back of the board pivots as you push it, or one of the halves is pinched into the blade somehow, only one of those back teeth needs to grab the workpiece to set kickback in motion. And it happens in milliseconds, as the lifting action converts almost instantly to horizontal force aimed right at you. The projectile can hurt you, obviously, but it can also pull your hand into the blade. The good news is that kickback is easy to prevent.

Use a splitter whenever possible—Also called a spreader or riving knife, a splitter keeps a board from making contact with the teeth at the back of the blade. Problem solved? Not exactly. The splitter has to be there to do its job, and until recently, most splitters were downright inconvenient and were therefore discarded. North American saws that are more than a few years old will have a crude splitter that extends high above the blade and too far behind it. The main problem is that these splitters have to come off the saw for all non-through-cuts, such as grooves. The big blade covers are just as inconvenient.

This outdated safety equipment is difficult to detach and reinstall, so most of these splitter/blade cover assemblies find a permanent home in a shop cabinet. If you have one of these saws, you still owe it to yourself to use a splitter (see "Older Saw? You Have Options," p. 19).

Three Core Principles

Staying safe begins with these three core concepts. No. 2 is specific to the tablesaw, but the others are critical on any piece of machinery.

1. Maintain Control

Never cut stock freehand. The stock must be controlled at all times, using either a fence or a jig. For this to work, miter slots and fences must be aligned properly. Also, a workpiece must be straight and flat on its control surfaces: at least one face and one edge. Be sure to push it all the way past the blade.

2. Use a Splitter

Kickback is the primary danger on a tablesaw, and a splitter is the cure. Also called a spreader or riving knife, this thin tab of metal or wood sits right behind the blade. The slot (kerf) made by the blade slides onto the splitter, preventing the board from pivoting onto the teeth at the back of the blade. Without having to steer the board to prevent kickback, you can focus on keeping your hands out of harm's way.

3. Limit Your Exposure to the Blade

Keep the blade only about ¼ in. higher than the workpiece. Whenever possible, keep the cover attached to the splitter, acting as a physical barrier. Keep your fingers 3 in. away from the cover, or 6 in. away from the exposed blade. For many cuts, this means using push sticks or push pads.

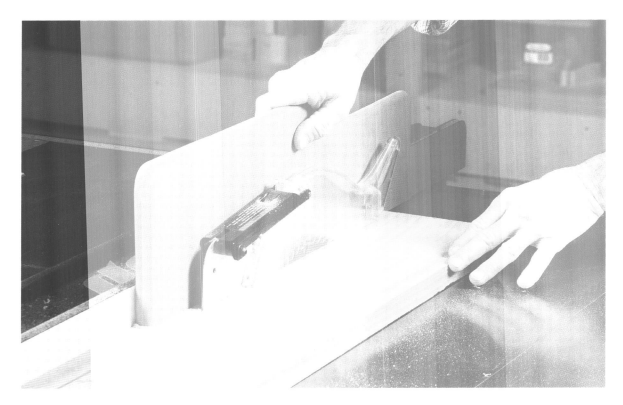

Today's saws have better guards. Years back, Underwriters Laboratories determined that all saws sold in the United States must have improved, European-style safety features, and all North American manufacturers did so.

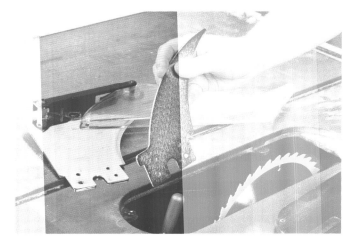

Better blade covers and splitters. New blade covers are narrower, allowing a push stick to pass by more easily (top photo). And the riving knife (photo above), an improved type of splitter, moves up and down with the blade, hugging it closely. The previous generation of

...cover knives is **a blessing**—Fortunately, a few years ago Underwriters Laboratories (UL®) proposed that all new tablesaws have a riving knife, a more versatile type of splitter borrowed from European tablesaws, and all of the North American tablesaw manufacturers complied.

If you can afford to buy a new saw, you'll find safety much more convenient. The riving knife can stay on for almost every type of cut, and the new blade covers are narrower and come off the saw more easily when they get in the way. Unfortunately, today's riving knives still include "anti-kickback fingers," which are basically useless and often in the way, so I remove them.

One gray area is getting your riving knife or splitter to fit through a shopmade throat plate. On my saw, I just extend the blade slot (using my scrollsaw) to allow the low-profile riving knife to fit through (see p. 23). But the taller knife won't work because it is longer,

(Continued on p. 22)

Low-profile option. For very thin rips (left) and non-through-cuts (right), the blade cover comes off easily, and you can either adjust the riving knife downward or replace it quickly with a low-profile version (bottom photo facing page).

Older Saw? You Have Options

Older splitter systems are inconvenient, and often discarded. But no worries—there are two good ways to replace them.

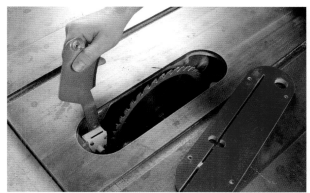

Buy a better splitter. Available online as an "Anti-Kickback Snap-In Spreader," the Biesemeyer® aftermarket splitter was designed for Delta® saws but works in many others. You install its holder in the throat of your saw, and then the splitter pops in and out quickly.

Or make a stub splitter. This little tab of wood goes into the saw slot (top) on a shopmade throat plate (see p. 23 for how to make one), and can be cut short so it works for non-through-cuts too (above). You'll need to lengthen the saw slot to accommodate it. If it binds in the sawkerf, just sand or plane the sides a bit. Be sure the grain runs vertically for strength.

Set Up for Safety

When ripping boards, you need the
fence to be parallel to the blade,
and you need a few shopmade
push sticks on hand.

Rip fence is easy to correct. Use the
adjustment screws to align the fence
with a miter slot, and it should stay
parallel in any position.

Align the Saw in Two Steps

How you adjust the table is different on
different saws, but you need the miter slots to
be parallel to the blade for safe crosscutting.
Then you adjust the rip fence parallel with the
slots and you're set for ripping, too.

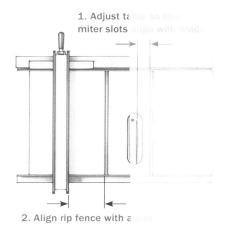

1. Adjust table so that
miter slots align with blade

2. Align rip fence with a slot

Smart Push Stick Design

The author's push sticks hook over the back
of a board, of course, but also extend over
the top of it for full control. He makes them in
MDF in a number of sizes and thicknesses.

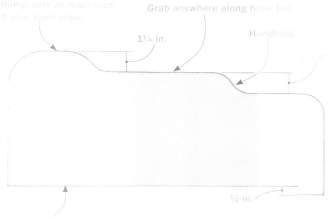

Bump acts as insurance
if your hand slips.

Grab anywhere along here, too

1¼ in.

Handhold

½ in.

Standard version thick by 8 in. tall by 18 in. long

Safe Ripping Is a 3-Step Process

Start the cut with your hands (1), as a push stick could tip the back of the board down and the front up. When your back hand is within 6 in. of the blade, stop pushing for a moment and grab the push stick (2), keeping the board stable with your left. Finish the cut (3) with the push stick, moving your left hand safely out of the way and pushing the stock all the way past the blade. Note how the outfeed table supports the board, so you don't have to.

Good Body Position

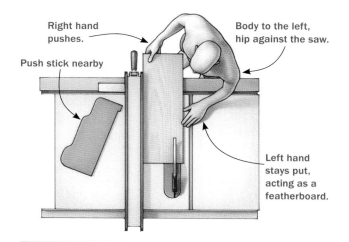

Right hand pushes.

Push stick nearby

Body to the left, hip against the saw.

Left hand stays put, acting as a featherboard.

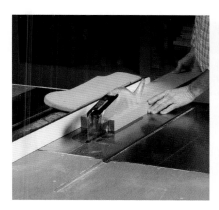

1

2

3

How to handle plywood. Focus on the area where the panel rides the rip fence, but remain aware of your hands, too, keeping them clear of the blade. Again, outfeed support is critical.

Crosscut basics: Set up for safety. Crosscuts produce the most tearout at the bottom edge, and a zero-clearance insert will prevent it. It will also keep small offcuts from dropping into the throat of the saw.

and I'd have to make the slot so long it would weaken the insert plate. So I use my zero-clearance throat plate for crosscutting only, where tearout is the biggest problem and where I need to use my low-profile knife anyway to fit through the fence on my miter gauge and crosscut sled. For ripping, I use the standard throat plate. That lets me use the full-height riving knife and blade cover.

A few more tips

Even if a board is already jointed straight and flat, it might not stay that way as internal tensions are released during a cut. If a board jams during the cut, use one hand to turn off the saw, wait for the blade to stop, and finish the cut on the bandsaw. Also, be aware that

a short board is more likely to pivot onto the back of the blade. If you are not sure about a workpiece, rip it on the bandsaw. And on some smaller, portable saws, the rip fence won't stay parallel to the blade when you move it, which can cause binding, so you'll need to check it each time.

One no-no when crosscutting is using the rip fence as a stop. This traps the offcut, and the friction against the fence can cause it to pivot and bind, causing kickback. For the rest of my safety rules, see the photos and illustrations throughout this chapter.

Follow these basic safety guidelines and you'll turn the most dangerous machine in the shop into a trusted friend.

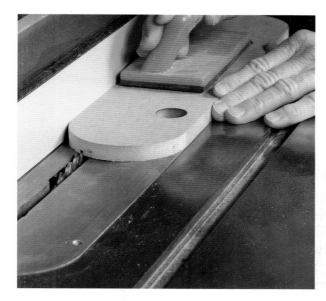

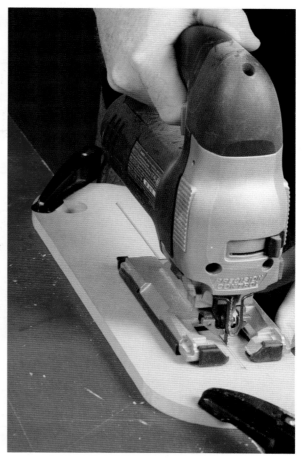

Make a zero-clearance throat insert. Trace your stock insert plate onto a piece of MDF (facing page) of the right thickness to fit your saw, and then bandsaw it close, using a sander to work up to the line. On most saws, a 10-in.-dia. blade won't go low enough to let you insert the blank plate, so make a ripcut along the bottom to create clearance (top). Then install the blank insert, place the rip fence on top of it, and bring the spinning blade up through it (above left). Last, extend the slot with a jigsaw (above right) or scrollsaw to accommodate your splitter or riving knife. You might also need to use tape or screws underneath to shim the plate level with the table.

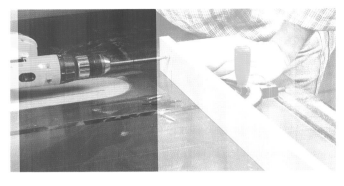 

Make a miter-gauge fence. A standard miter gauge is of some help. A long fence will improve control, support the workpiece on the back edge, and push the offcut safely past the blade. Screw a long piece of MDF to your miter gauge with a few holes, and then attach a wood block (as shown in the next step) where the blade emerges.

Stick trick. The slots in your outfeed table, designed to accommodate miter gauges and sled runners, are the perfect spot for a lumber stick that limits their travel, making sure the stock can't pass through the safety block (or box) at the back of the fence.

Accurate crosscutting. Zero clearance is your friend. After cutting one end of the stock square, mark the length at the other end, and line the slot in your miter-gauge fence up to the mark.

Set the stop. The long MDF auxiliary fence lets you set a stop at the far end for cutting a series of workpieces to the same length.

Perfect support. With a big, stable bed riding in the miter-gauge slots, a shop-built sled cuts big workpieces with impressive accuracy. Again, you can clamp stops to the fence. For wide workpieces, clamp a block-type stop above the workpiece.

Tips for Square Glue-Ups

STEVE LATTA

The absolute worst time to try to solve a problem is when the glue is starting to tack. I watch my students scurry like mice in a maze, tracking down extra clamps to pull together a joint that just won't budge. In desperation, out comes the claw hammer and then things really start a downward slide.

Frantic glue-ups create open joints and out-of-square assemblies, which in turn means that doors and drawers don't fit. Sad to say, these wounds are usually self-inflicted. However, if you follow a few basic steps before and during the glue-up, you can approach this stressful time calmly and confidently.

Laying the foundation

First and foremost, gluing up a project needs to be viewed as the end of a process, not an isolated event. Proper alignment doesn't just magically happen, but rather is the outcome of a well-executed plan.

Let's start with design. For example, if I'm building a free-standing, open-front bookcase with fixed shelves, I'd feel comfortable using slats for the back. The glued shelves make up for the slats' lack of rigidity. However, if inset doors are part of the design, and if the shelves are adjustable, I'd go with a frame-and-panel back, especially one with glued-in panels. It will help make the main box square, which makes fitting the doors much easier. It also will keep it rigid, preventing the doors from binding.

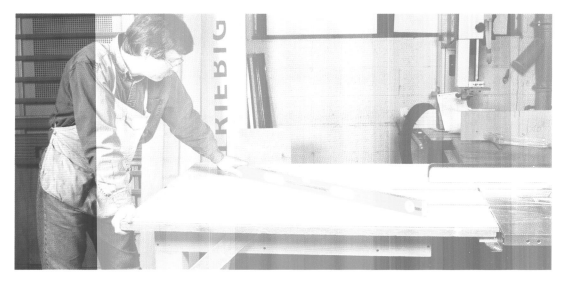

Get a good start. [...] glue-ups if the co[...] and the assembly [...] a 4-ft. level to see [...] table (top) is flat. [...] of ¾-in.-thick MDF [...] of sawhorses and [...] surface flat (above [...]

Equal parts. Parts on opposite sides of a piece [...] the length between shoulders t[...] [...] square corners.

You can't perform the impossible

It sounds obvious, but the piece you're gluing up should have the potential to be square! For example, if making a small table with a single drawer opening, the shoulder-to-shoulder distance on the rear apron better match the shoulder-to-shoulder distance on the drawer rails in the front. If not, the table will be a trapezoid and the joints may show gaps. Likewise, the shoulder-to-shoulder distance of the upper and lower drawer rails better be the same or the opening, no matter how much tweaking is involved, won't be square.

Make the Right Clamping Block

Direct the Pressure Where You Need It: Bad

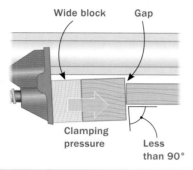

Wide block — Gap

Clamping pressure — Less than 90°

Too wide. Using a wide caul directs the force of the clamp to the front of this leg, twisting it out of parallel with the rear apron.

Direct the Pressure Where You Need It: Good

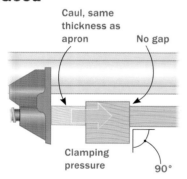

Caul, same thickness as apron — No gap

Clamping pressure — 90°

Direct the force. A clamping block the same thickness as the apron and placed in line with it (left) keeps the leg straight (right). Tape the cauls in place to leave your hands free for clamping.

Gap-Free Face Frame

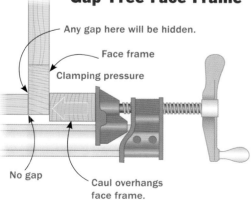

Any gap here will be hidden.

Face frame

Clamping pressure

No gap

Caul overhangs face frame.

Gap-free face frame. The visible outside of the face frame must join seamlessly with the carcase; the hidden inner side of the joint is less critical. To direct the clamping force to the outside, place the caul so that it overhangs the exterior of the cabinet.

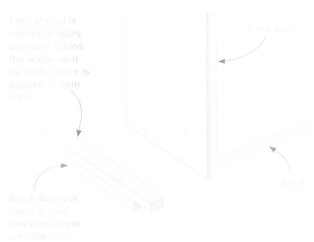

Each of caul is
convex to apply
pressure across
the whole joint
as clamp force is
applied at both
ends.

Caul ends

Stock

Block turned or
glued to caul
elevates it even
with the joint

Two clamps, two cauls, two hands. To spread
the pressure where clamps can't reach, put a
convex curve on the face of a caul to get even
pressure across a wide joint. Elevating the caul
on a block of wood brings it level with the joint,
leaving your hands free to use the clamps.

Have good-fitting joints and use the right cauls

Joints that fit properly need minimal
clamping pressure. If an assembly can only
come square by overtightening the clamps,
the object will not remain square when the
clamps come off but will eventually creep
back into distortion.

You should prepare properly sized clamping blocks and cauls to direct the pressure
accurately. Grabbing random-size blocks
misdirects the pressure and just doesn't get
the job done. For larger cases, corner braces
with clamp holes along the edge ensure 90°
corners.

Tools to check for squareness

A combination square is useful for checking
to see if corners are 90°. For larger pieces,
plastic 30°–60°–90° corner drafting triangles
come in a variety of sizes. However, even
if a corner is 90°, the piece as a whole can
be out of square. Measuring the diagonal

distances is a foolproof way to check. A tape
measure works great for exterior corner-
to-corner dimensions. However, if clamps
are obscuring the exterior corners, you can
measure the interior diagonals using two
sliding sticks with ends cut to a point.

Practice makes perfect

The number one rule that should never, ever
be ignored: Always do a complete dry-fit with
all clamps, blocks, and corner supports. If
you can't get the piece square during a dry-fit,
you'll never get it square with the actual glue.

After a bad rehearsal, actors may com-
ment, "It'll be all right on the night," but for
woodworkers, all the lines must be perfect
before the glue is applied.

Four Ways to Check for Square

1. Combo square. A combination square is a great tool to check that corners are square in small openings.

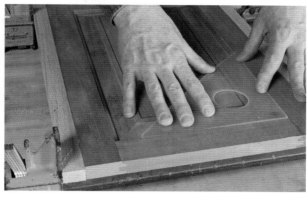

2. Flexible choice. A raised panel may interfere with a rigid square but a plastic triangle can be bent downward to contact the frame.

3. Check diagonals. Make your clamping cauls shorter than the sides so that you can hook a tape measure over the corner and measure each diagonal. They should be within ⅛ in. of each other.

4. Check inside. If clamps are blocking the outside corners, you can check the interior diagonals using two sliding sticks with pointed ends (right). Measure the first diagonal and draw a line across both sticks. Then measure the opposite diagonal.

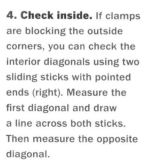

Move the ends of clamps that are near the longer diagonal out toward the corners.

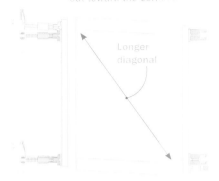

Longer diagonal

Two ways to adjust: Angle the clamps. If the diagonals are different lengths, shift the clamps to pull the frame into alignment.

POWERMAT

Or add corner braces. Clamping a square brace across one of the corners can bring the entire assembly back to square.

BUILT-INS

Built-In Corner Seating Nook

M y friends Debbie and Tom decided to make better use of a small room next to their kitchen. They wanted a built-in seat that could serve as an informal dining area and a place for board games or homework.

After measuring the space and designing the seat in cross section, I made a SketchUp® model of a seat with enough room for four people, storage drawers below, and a cabinet in the back of the corner seat. Before I started building, I made a 24-in.-wide plywood mock-up to make sure it would be comfortable. We agreed that the mock-up was more comfortable with a ¾-in. plywood block under the front edge. I gave the seat an additional 5° tilt, then made a new SketchUp model of the base of the seat.

Because I would be working alone, building the seat in the shop and installing it as a complete unit were out of the question. Even if I had the strength to do so, the house was built in the 18th century, so plumb, level, and square had long since vanished. Because there was sure to be lots of scribing and fitting before the seat was in place, it made sense to break down the job into manageable parts. I decided to start with a level plinth, then to install the base as four separate boxes. Next, I would install the seat and the corner-cabinet unit, and then finish up with all of the solid-wood parts (the seat back, nosings, and moldings). I could make all the parts in the shop, then assemble everything together at the house.

The Critical Angles

Unlike a built-in or a set of stairs, a bench might look fine on paper, but the real test is whether it feels comfortable. A short mock-up built of plywood gives both the designer and the client a good sense of the bench's ergonomics.

Seat back is beveled at 5° at the bottom and 15° at the top.

25 in.

39 in.

95°

16 in.

Seat angled up 10°

Seat front angled 10° back for legroom

6¼ in.

17 in.

3½ in.

22⅝ in.

A scribe may be necessary. Position the opposite side base and check the fit. Use a set of scribes to mark the cut.

Build boxes to form the seat

For the boxes below the seat, I used dimensions from the SketchUp model to cut parts from ¾-in. birch plywood. Because the seat has a 10° pitch, the joint between the cabinets at the top is a compound miter. To cut the joints, I used a circular saw with the blade set to a 3.81° bevel and a shooting board. (The bevel angle came from a chart I found online at www.woodshoptips.com/ tips/012003/012003.pdf.) I cut the corner cabinet to the dimensions on the SketchUp model, but I made the two adjoining cabinets 1 in. longer so that I would have room to scribe and fit the joints in place.

Next, using a dado and rabbet joint that was glued and nailed, I made drawers from ½-in. Baltic-birch plywood. I delayed making

A saw guide is a must. When trimming scribed cuts, a site-built saw guide is a fast way to make an accurate cut.

Join Base Units with a Compound Angle

Begin with a level framework of plinth boxes. The plywood seat bases sit atop the plinth boxes and will eventually house drawers. Because the seat is angled back the corner boxes are joined with a 22.5° angle and an approximately 4° bevel.

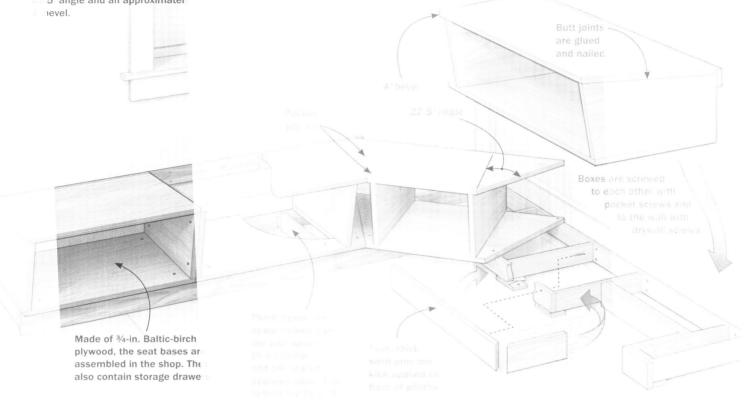

Butt joints are glued and nailed

4° bevel

22.5° angle

Pocket screw

Boxes are screwed to each other with pocket screws and to the wall with drywall screws

Made of ¾-in. Baltic-birch plywood, the seat bases are assembled in the shop. They also contain storage drawers.

Plinth boxes are made to look like the toe space of a cabinet and are placed approximately 1 in. behind the face of the seat.

1-in.-thick solid-pine toe kick applied to front of plinths

the applied drawer fronts until the boxes and the face frames were in place and I could get an accurate measurement.

While in the shop, I ripped ¾-in. pine plywood to 16 in. for the seats. The back just overlaps the back edge of the seat. I also milled other parts, such as the solid-pine roundover nosing for the seat, the pine grooved paneling, the face frame, and the cap stock.

Playing by old-house rules

Once on-site, my first task was to install the plinth, which is essentially a plywood box 3½ in. high that is analogous to a cabinet's toe kick. Starting at the high point, I leveled each side across, shimming with blocks and screwing the base to the baseboard. I hid the plywood and the gaps with a 1× pine kick board that I scribed to the floor.

The corner base unit was next. I marked left and right reference points an equal distance from the inside corner, then centered the corner base between the two points and screwed it to the plinth. Next, I scribed each of the flanking base units to the corner, checked the fit, and pocket-screwed the top edges together. I also screwed them together at the sides and into the walls.

The next part of the puzzle was the corner seat back (see the drawing on p. 36). Built in the shop, the unit doubles as a storage cabinet. The idea was to use the storage unit as a reference when it came time to frame the rest of the seat back. I positioned the corner unit so that it was parallel to the front and level, then toe-screwed it to the seat and to the wall.

I opted to fit and install the plywood seat panels first, then have the seat back land on the seat. Otherwise, I'd have to scribe the seat to the back, leaving a visible joint. Beveled to the same angles as the seat base, the panels were ripped at 16 in. wide and cut to length to form an equal overhang at the front and sides. I attached the panels with screws driven up through the base.

The seat-back frame is a custom fit

Because the walls were not flat or plumb, I began making the seat-back frame with a series of triangular plywood panels connected by 1×4s. Notched over a ledger, the triangles' bases were screwed to the seat bases. Next, I attached horizontal 1×4s across the top, middle, and bottom as nailers for the beadboard seat back. After both sides were complete, I covered the corner unit with a face frame.

Once these parts were fit and nailed up, I filled in the rest of the seat back, choosing the appropriate widths to fit the space. The right side went quickly, but the left was complicated by a window (see the drawing on p. 36). There, I had to notch the first piece and lower a few more to make room for a small shelf below the windowsill.

When the back was complete, I glued and nailed the nosing to the front and side edges of the seat (see the drawing on pp. 38–39). Below the seat, I covered the veneer edges of the plywood with 1× solid stock, then filled in the face frames in the corners and above the drawers. After mounting the drawers on full-extension slides, I cut and fit the drawer fronts. Then I finished the beadboard paneling on the ends of the unit and added the final face-frame piece.

To cap it off, I started with a piece of ¾-in. pine plywood, which I fit into the corner by tick-sticking (a boatbuilder's scribing technique for fitting a board into an irregularly shaped recess). I then scribed solid cap pieces to the wall along each side, butting them to the side of the plywood and mitering them where they met the nosing on the front edge. I hung the doors on the corner unit with full-overlay cup hinges and fit a quirked bead against the face frame around them. Finally, I cleaned up my pencil marks and finish-sanded the unit. After I left, the painter came in and applied oil-based stain, sealed it with a coat of shellac, and brushed on two coats of polyurethane.

Cap Things Off with Solid Pine

The seat back and sides are covered with solid-pine beadboard milled in the shop. The gap on each side of the window casing is filled with the same stock. The plywood cap is scribed in place on the corner cabinet and butted to the solid-pine cap stock that runs along the back. Solid-pine nosings hide plywood edges.

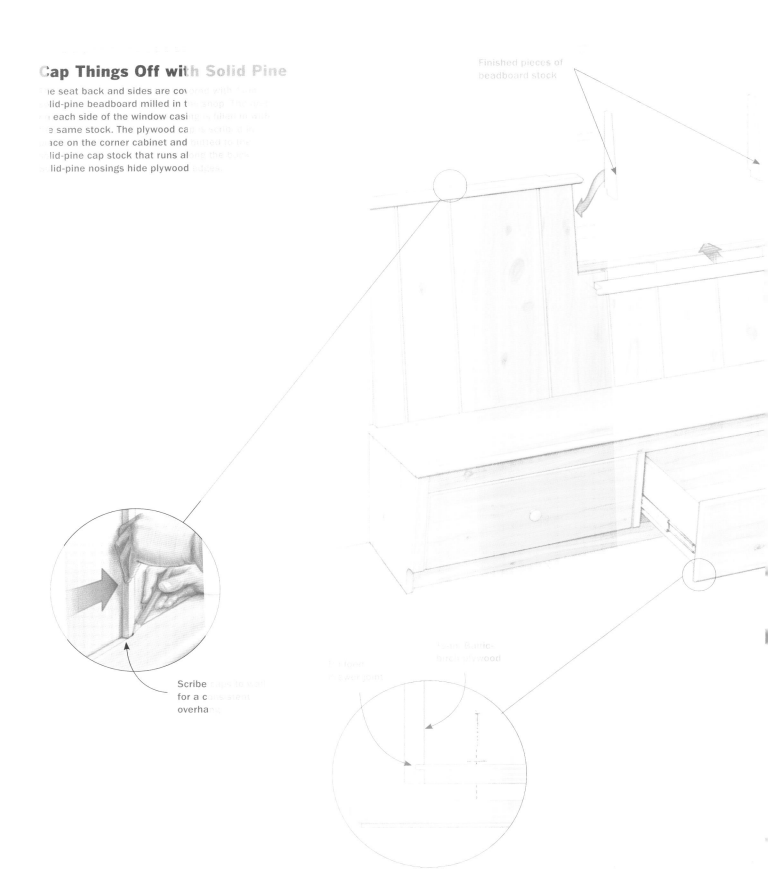

Finished pieces of beadboard stock

Scribe ... to wall for a consistent overhang

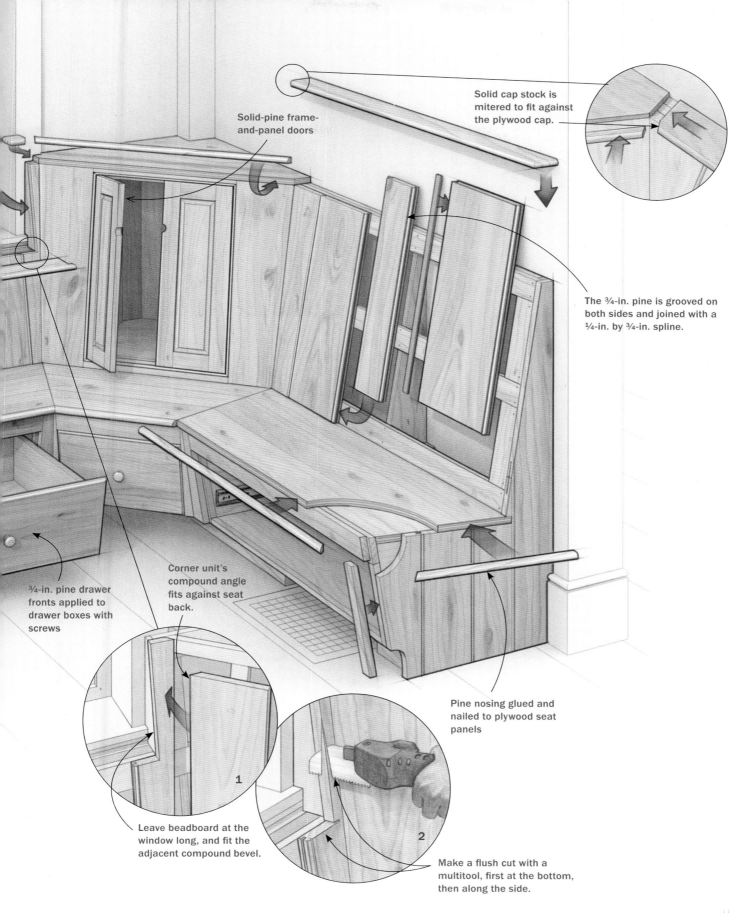

Solid-pine frame-and-panel doors

Solid cap stock is mitered to fit against the plywood cap.

The ¾-in. pine is grooved on both sides and joined with a ¼-in. by ¾-in. spline.

¾-in. pine drawer fronts applied to drawer boxes with screws

Corner unit's compound angle fits against seat back.

Pine nosing glued and nailed to plywood seat panels

1

Leave beadboard at the window long, and fit the adjacent compound bevel.

2

Make a flush cut with a multitool, first at the bottom, then along the side.

Find the angle. The corner unit's beadboard intersects at a compound angle. From the edge of the face frame, measure top and bottom.

Install the beadboard from the corner out. Starting to the right of the bottom of the corner unit, nail the first board on a plumb line.

Fit the board. After cutting the compound angle with a saw guide, nail it against the first board. After repeating the process on the other side of the corner unit, fill in the rest of the boards out to the ends.

Comfortable Dining Nooks

JOSEPH LANZA

When space is tight, a built-in dining nook can provide many benefits. It can do double duty by including built-in storage, and it can save money (and decisions) by reducing the need for furniture. In new construction, that can help you to build smaller. If you are remodeling, a nook can make use of awkward, small, or difficult spaces. On top of all these practical advantages, a well-designed nook feels good to be in; it provides the deep architectural pleasure that comes when a space is crafted to accommodate its human uses.

Location is first

Just like designing a house, designing a good nook starts with the site. Proximity to the food-prep area is important, but the primary concerns are traffic patterns and light. Locate the nook out of the way of major thoroughfares, if possible. The seating should be easy to get in and out of. Restaurant-style booths don't work well without waitstaff. "Captive" seats should have more than one way out, not including crawling under the table (see the top left drawing on p. 43). This generally limits built-in seating to two sides of a rectangular table or 180° of a round table.

The sun is always the best source of light. If possible, locate the nook near windows, and incorporate those windows into the design of the nook (see the drawing on p. 42). Be sure to use tempered glass if the windows are within reach of elbows. East- or south-facing windows are best for daylight. Also, consider any existing or potential views to the outside. If there is nothing worth seeing outside, consider interior views of adjacent rooms and architectural features.

Artificial lighting should be planned not just for dining but also for table activities such as work, games, and crafts. Provide ambient as well as direct overhead light, making sure to locate fixtures to avoid glare at seated eye level. Dimmers on all fixtures will allow light to be adjusted for a wide range of activities.

Comfort comes next

Once the big questions of location, layout, and lighting are settled, it's time to move to the ergonomics of the seat itself. There is no need to reinvent the seat. You might start with a bit of empirical research, trying out restaurant booths until you find a comfortable one, then measuring it. If you don't find one quickly, this method could get expensive, though enjoyable as long as the food is better than the seating.

There is a lot of anthropometric data out there. Because a lot of industries depend on it, I was surprised to find that not much solid information is available online. The American Institute of Architects' *Architectural Graphic Standards*, 12th ed. (Wiley & Sons, 2016), probably has enough to get you started on a comfortable design, but the best source I know of is *Humanscale* 1/2/3 (MIT Press, 1974). This portfolio contains a booklet with anthropometric measurements, a comprehensive list of seating-design considerations, a discussion of design requirements for the handicapped and elderly, and three pictorial selectors containing rotary dials that give specific dimensions for designing for people of various sizes. Unfortunately, it is now out of print. The bottom drawing on the facing page shows how I applied *Humanscale* dimensions to a particular project.

If you plan to use seat cushions, 1 in. to 2 in. of firm padding is plenty. Don't lower the seat by much, because the foam will compress. Lumbar support is an important feature for long-term seating comfort, but I usually ignore it for built-ins. Properly curved lumbar support would require bending plywood or horizontal slats (coopered or butted) for the back rest. Throw pillows are simpler and more cost-effective.

After arriving at a design in cross section, make a mock-up about 24 in. wide. I did this for the seat shown on p. 32. I had started with a seat pitch of 5°. However, test sitters found the seat more comfortable when angled back about 5° more, so I adjusted the angle.

Once you have a comfortable seat, consider storage. The table usually will make access to any space under the seat a bit awkward, so it's better to make the access from the ends (see the top right drawing on the facing page). If that does not work for your layout, try drawers under the seat. A lift-up seat is easier to build but awkward to use. The space behind the seat backs is usually easier to get to, and the seat backs can be doors that are hinged on the sides or at the bottom. If there is enough room, the seat backs can be made deeper to accommodate more storage. If your seat makes a diagonal corner in a square room, a corner cabinet behind it can hold a lot of stuff.

Corner Seat at 45°

Corners often make good sites for nooks, but square corners create dead spots that are not useful for seating. If there is enough space, it is usually better to cross the corner with a seat at 45° to the two sides. This is the approach the author used in "Built-In Corner Seating Nook" on p. 32. It usually works best with a round or oval table, and it requires a relatively wide space for the nook.

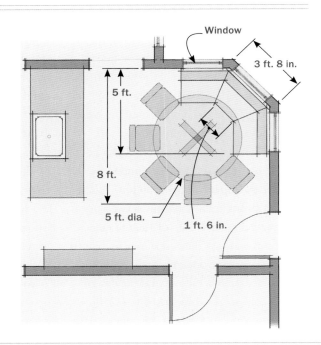

Window

3 ft. 8 in.

5 ft.

8 ft.

5 ft. dia.

1 ft. 6 in.

L-Shaped Corner Seat

If the space you've chosen for your dining nook is narrow, leave the corner open so that the person in the corner on the long side of the table has some elbow room, as well as two ways to get out.

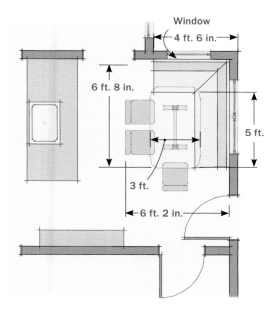

Booth with Two Open Ends

If your dining area does not have a suitable corner, a built-in bench on one side of a table will work. You also might use a kitchen island or other architectural element to create a booth with two open ends.

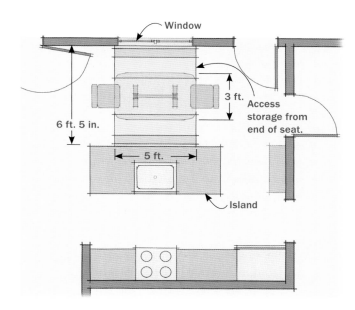

Calculating Comfort

For this seat, the author used the *Humanscale* seat/table guide selector and dialed in the numbers for an average male or tall female (5 ft. 9 in. when the book was published in 1974). The critical points are the height at the front of the seat (about 17 in.); the length of the seat (16 in. provides thigh support without hitting the back of the knee); the pitch of the seat (a minimum of 5°); the angle of the seat back (95°); and the height of the backrest (a minimum of 16 in. to support the thoracic region, or "chicken wings"). Finally, the front of the seat should slope back so that no one will whack the backs of their legs.

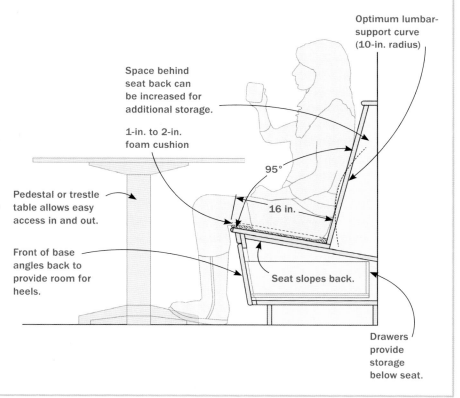

Built-In Breakfast Nook

ANDREW YOUNG

Built-ins add functionality to any space, but few types offer as much day-in and day-out utility as a breakfast nook. For this project, the client had a compact kitchen that didn't leave much room for a table and chairs. It was a space just begging for a breakfast nook.

A breakfast nook allows at least half of the seating around the table to be flat against the wall, eliminating the space needed behind chairs. It also allows the table to be tucked closer to the corner, opening up floor space, improving flow, and making the room feel bigger, all while offering additional storage. Unlike bookcases and window seats, a breakfast nook is a built-in that is likely to get daily use and abuse. So besides needing to be aesthetically pleasing, it has to be functionally designed and built to take a beating.

Dimensions to know

I've built enough breakfast nooks over the years to have a basic formula for dimensions. I usually aim for an 18-in. finished seat height, which includes cushions. Standard thickness for foam is 4 in., and I allow for about 2 in. of compression, so I usually design the bench so that the plywood below the cushions is 16 in. above the finished floor. For seat depth, I like 18 in. from the front lip to the lowest portion of the angled backrest. My designs don't typically include a cushioned backrest, but if yours does, you will need to adjust this number to account for the added thickness.

Benchmark Dimensions

Compared to other built-ins, a bench can be a challenge. These pieces need to look good, feel good, provide usable storage, and integrate well with adjacent cabinetry, doors, and windows. Your design may vary based on style and the particulars of the room, but I've found these dimensions to be a good baseline.

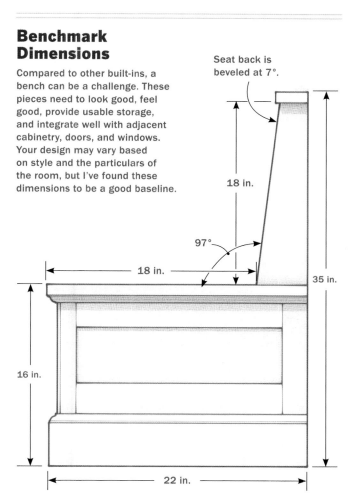

Seat back is beveled at 7°.

18 in.

97°

18 in.

35 in.

16 in.

22 in.

While a straight back is easier to build (especially in a corner bench), a slight angle— 7° is what I used here—adds quite a bit of comfort and visual interest. If I'm tucking the built-in below a window, I prefer to use the window stool height as the top edge of the backrest, which in this case worked out to a comfortable 18 in. from the seat.

It's typical to include storage in this style of built-in—drawers in the side or end of the unit, or lids that lift off or are hinged. I find that drawers and slides eat up a lot of storage space, so I prefer hinged lids.

With the critical dimensions and site specifics noted, I can flesh out the design and then begin fabricating parts in the shop.

Shop fabrication

The heart of this assembly is the plywood carcases, which not only serve as the storage areas but are the main components onto which the rest of the assembly is fastened.

I like the interior to be as presentable as the exterior, so I use prefinished cabinet-grade maple plywood for the carcases— ¾ in. thick for the sides and back, ½ in. thick for the bottom—which also eliminates the need for painting the interior. I break the carcases into at least two equal sections (more for long runs) to ensure ample support. I generally avoid going more than 48 in. without adding a vertical support; for this project, a single center divider was sufficient. In the case of a corner unit such as this one, you also need to decide which carcase is going to run long into the corner. I usually run the shorter of the two benches into the corner.

In order to maintain the illusion of a true furniture leg, I set a recessed base assembly 6 in. from the front face. That's far enough back so that you can't see it, but shallow enough so that you can reach dust bunnies and runaway Cheerios®. The base assembly is made from ¾-in. plywood but is later skinned over with ¼-in. MDF, so it provides a good opportunity to use scrap that has accumulated in the shop.

I build all of the bench-frame components with paint-grade European beech, which isn't quite as soft as poplar but is easier to work than maple. Frames are assembled with pocket screws and are built a little oversize to allow for scribing and unknown site conditions. The same goes for the furniture legs; I cut the decorative curves in the shop but let the ends run long, leaving me wiggle room once I get to the site.

The frame-and-panel treatment on the front of the carcases includes a rabbet for the plywood panel, which goes up against the storage carcase and can therefore be glued

Anticipate the unknown.
Although many of the bench
parts are fabricated in the
shop, all face frames, bracket
feet, and moldings are left
oversize to be cut and/or
scribed on-site for a perfect fit.

and pinned to the frame rather than acting as
a true floating panel.

To ensure purposeful reveals and proportions, I factor in the width of any moldings I
plan to apply to the boxes once installed. For
corner units, I need to consider which side of
the front frame and furniture feet will overlap the other at the inside corner. I've learned
that if I don't address these matters during
the design and shop-fabrication stages, those
oversights will haunt me when I'm on-site.

At the job site

Once I'm on-site, my first step is to remove
millwork and other obstacles, such as
electrical devices, which are never OK to
leave energized if they are to be buried
behind a permanent piece of furniture. Next,
I mark all the studs in the area by drawing
vertical lines on the wall; this reduces the
need to hunt them out one at a time later in
the process. A little time on the front end
saves me a lot in the long run.

I start the actual installation with the
storage carcases, which are assembled in the
shop with the recessed bases attached. Since
all components are built off these boxes, it's
imperative that they be installed dead level,
plumb, and square to each other (in the case
of a corner installation).

With the carcases in place, I add the solid-
wood frame components—first the frame that
will support the lids, and then the frames and
panels that dress up the front and sides.

The 7° back assembly is supported by a pair
of angled nailers cut from quality, kiln-dried
2× stock. The upper nailer is attached to the
wall just below the sill, and the lower nailer
is fastened to a lid cleat that's on top of the
carcases below. Spanning the nailers is ¾-in.
CDX plywood, which creates a stiff subbase
for another pocket-screw frame that is then
infilled with solid-wood tongue-and-groove
paneling for a traditional look.

(Continued on p. 50)

Make way for the cap. If tying the bench seat into a windowsill, strike a level line across the window casing. Cut along the line with a handsaw or multitool, and remove the molding.

Help shims stay put. Stack shims to fit, then remove and coat with glue. Reinsert the stacks, let the glue dry, and trim the stacks flush.

Wedges before shims. Reusable oak wedges are larger and steeper than typical shims, making them ideal for quickly and temporarily getting carcases into position before shims are added.

Boxes Create a Foundation

As with any cabinet installation, time spent getting the assembled plywood carcases level, flush along their top edges, and square to each other at the corner pays dividends when installing the components that come afterward.

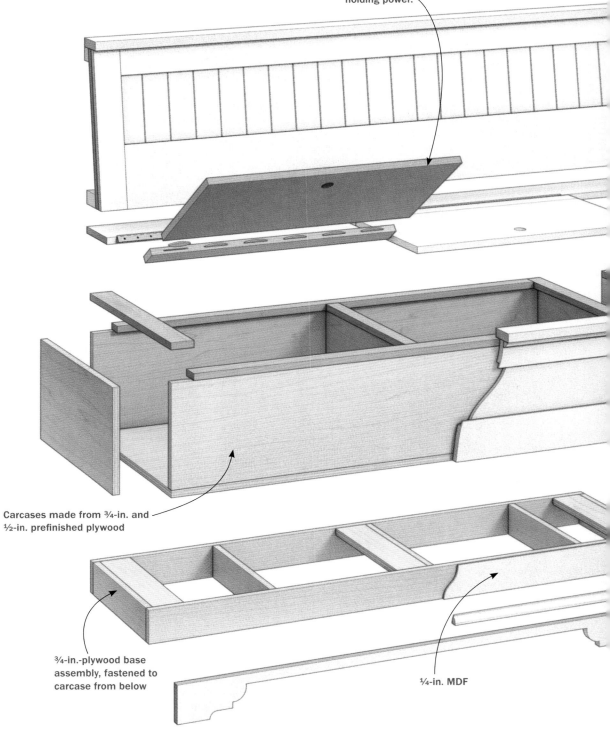

¾-in. MDF panels with hardwood edges provide smooth, clean-edge lids with improved hinge-screw holding power.

Carcases made from ¾-in. and ½-in. prefinished plywood

¾-in.-plywood base assembly, fastened to carcase from below

¼-in. MDF

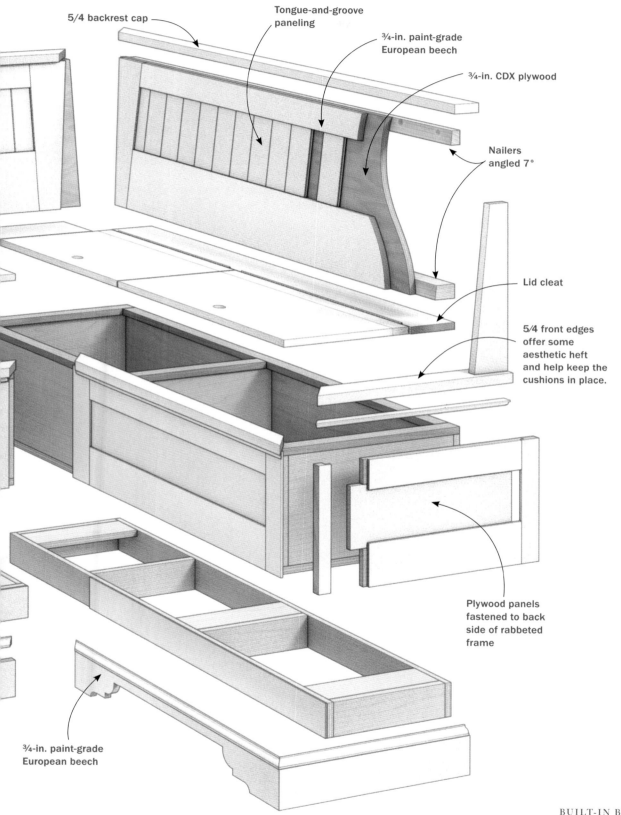

5/4 backrest cap

Tongue-and-groove paneling

¾-in. paint-grade European beech

¾-in. CDX plywood

Nailers angled 7°

Lid cleat

5/4 front edges offer some aesthetic heft and help keep the cushions in place.

Plywood panels fastened to back side of rabbeted frame

¾-in. paint-grade European beech

Flush it up. Set the top frames in glue, and align all outside edges flush to the face of the carcases before fastening with finish nails.

Skin the boxes. Trim each front panel to length, and fasten it to the carcase face with finish nails.

Lid cleat does heavy lifting. This 1x6, referenced off the front edge of the carcase, supports the backrest assembly and the lid hinges.

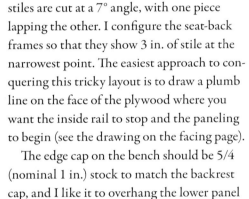

Window locates the top nailer. I like to align the bench back with the windowsill, which usually means removing part of the existing casing and making a new, deeper stool. Clamp the backrest cap in place to set the height of the angled top nailer, then screw the nailer to the wall at each stud location.

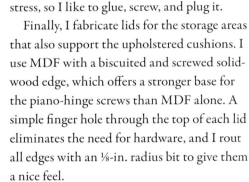

On the inside corner of the seatback, both stiles are cut at a 7° angle, with one piece lapping the other. I configure the seat-back frames so that they show 3 in. of stile at the narrowest point. The easiest approach to conquering this tricky layout is to draw a plumb line on the face of the plywood where you want the inside rail to stop and the paneling to begin (see the drawing on the facing page).

The edge cap on the bench should be 5/4 (nominal 1 in.) stock to match the backrest cap, and I like it to overhang the lower panel by 1 in. or so. This piece tends to see a lot of stress, so I like to glue, screw, and plug it.

Finally, I fabricate lids for the storage areas that also support the upholstered cushions. I use MDF with a biscuited and screwed solid-wood edge, which offers a stronger base for the piano-hinge screws than MDF alone. A simple finger hole through the top of each lid eliminates the need for hardware, and I rout all edges with an ⅛-in. radius bit to give them a nice feel.

The lids are best left loose until after the whole bench has been painted, which allows the painters access without having to work around the piano hinges.

Beveled backrest. To create a sturdy backrest subbase, fasten ¾-in. CDX plywood with top and bottom bevels to the upper and lower nailers.

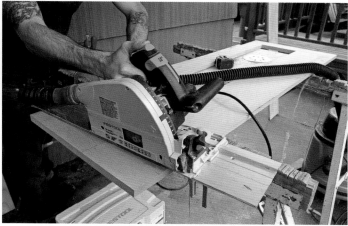

Seven on a bevel. Cut the seat-back frame along the 7° line, adding a slight back bevel to ensure a tight fit along the show side of the joint.

The base follows the box. Shim up and scab onto the bracket feet as necessary to keep an even reveal on an out-of-level floor.

Accurate angles. Adjust the bottom nailer in or out at each screw location until a digital level reads 83°—a perfect 7° slope—before fastening the nailer to the lid cleat below.

The Trick for a Tapered Stile

For the backrest panel frame, start with an extrawide stile on one end to allow for the tapered cut necessary to meet the adjacent piece in the corner. I prefer to see 3 in. of stile at the narrowest visible point, which matches the width of the straight-cut stiles. To get an accurate measurement for this tricky spot, do your layout and take your measurements on the plywood.

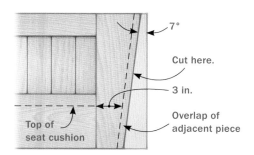

7°

Cut here.

3 in.

Overlap of adjacent piece

Top of seat cushion

Tongue-and-groove symmetry. To dress up the benches and enhance their built-in, furniture-type look, I apply tongue-and-groove paneling to the backs, traditional furniture-style legs to the lower boxes, and simple detail moldings to ease some of the transitions between pieces. Cut each piece of paneling with a 2° bevel at top and bottom to ensure a tight fit between rails, then dry-fit them and adjust the whole row of pieces until the gaps at the ends are equal. With the end pieces cut to width, fasten each board with pin nails.

The hinge sets the gap. After coming close to the final lid dimensions, set the lids in their openings with the piano hinge slid into place at the rear, then check and adjust the gap at the sides and front.

A perfect fit. Once painted and fitted with cushions, the finished bench looks right at home, adding hidden storage, flexible seating, and increased flow to a busy kitchen.

Design the Perfect Pantry

PAUL DEGROOT

Ask your neighbors what they dislike about their pantries, and you'll likely get an earful: "It's too small" or "I can't find anything in it." I hear these complaints on cue from clients. Clearly, the way we store our soup and cereal warrants careful planning.

Whether you are building a new kitchen or remodeling what you have, you need to consider what makes a pantry work and which kind is best for your situation. Here, I'll describe the three main types of pantries: cabinets, reach-ins, and walk-ins. I'll also offer a suggestion for a hybrid pantry/mudroom that the homeowners walk through as they enter the house. The drawings are meant to illustrate the basics; the photos show some of my actual projects.

Just keep two things in mind as you read and plan your pantry: Good design means keeping things simple, and the right location often trumps size. Sometimes, a hard-working cabinet is all you need for convenient access to all your kitchen goods.

The basics: Location and lighting

Convenience and visibility are the essential attributes of a great pantry. Regardless of size, the pantry should be in a handy location, positioned in the kitchen or immediately next to it. A modest pantry cabinet placed within the kitchen footprint will be more convenient for regular use than an oversize

Location, Location, Location

An efficient smaller kitchen has the pantry on one side of the stove, separated by about 4 ft. of counter, and the refrigerator on the other side of the stove, separated by a similar stretch of counter. Both sides of the stove are convenient prep zones. In larger kitchens, the pantry also should be near a working counter or an island and preferably near the doorway where groceries enter the home.

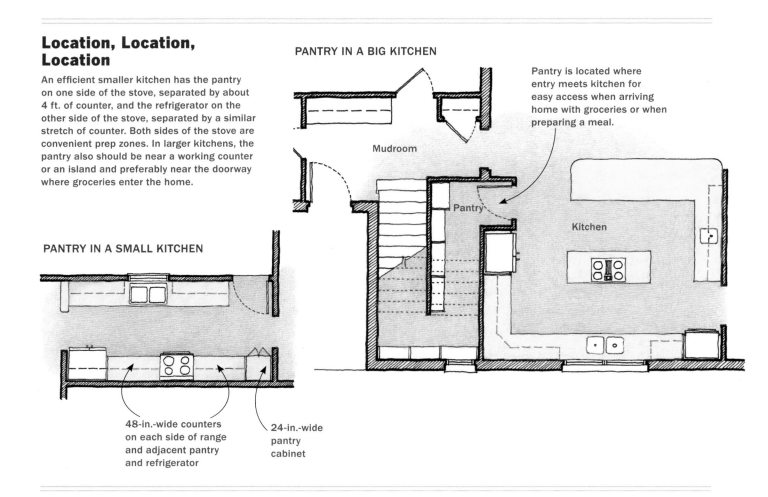

PANTRY IN A BIG KITCHEN

Pantry is located where entry meets kitchen for easy access when arriving home with groceries or when preparing a meal.

Mudroom

Pantry

Kitchen

PANTRY IN A SMALL KITCHEN

48-in.-wide counters on each side of range and adjacent pantry and refrigerator

24-in.-wide pantry cabinet

---

walk-in down the hall. Plus, every pantry's utility will be improved with counter space for sorting and unloading groceries.

Pantries also must have proper lighting so that you can see the contents well. Ceiling-mounted linear fluorescents work well for walk-in pantries. Install the fixtures parallel to the longest shelving runs for best light. Due to the extra cost, most of the cabinet pantries I design don't have internal lighting, so I make sure that there is adequate kitchen lighting directly outside the cabinet. Often, this means that I will locate one or two recessed fixtures about 16 in. from the face of the cabinet. A reach-in closet pantry will benefit from a low-profile fluorescent light mounted inside, especially when a tall header

blocks ambient light from the high shelves. I specify slim, no-frills fluorescents with rounded acrylic diffusers for these above-door applications.

Electrical codes are strict about the types and the locations of lights installed in closets. Treat pantry lighting with similar caution. If you must use incandescent fixtures, be sure to place them well away from any open shelves that might be packed with paper goods and combustibles.

A better pantry may not be bigger

Cabinet pantries are space efficient, typically occupying just 4 sq. ft. to 8 sq. ft. of floor area. For big families and others who buy in bulk, I sometimes supplement the in-kitchen pantry cabinet with a larger pantry elsewhere.

Reach-in closet pantries (see p. 58) range in size from 6 sq. ft. to 12 sq. ft., assuming a 24-in. depth and a width from 3 ft. to 6 ft. There are occasions where a 24-in. depth is not possible. In these cases, a 12-in. depth is the minimum, but 16 in. or more would allow some storage flexibility. It's difficult to see and access items at the extreme sides of a wide reach-in closet pantry with a narrow doorway. Except on the smallest of reach-ins, I use pairs of doors with the sidewalls of the closet no more than 6 in. from each door jamb.

Surrounded by 2×4 stud walls, pantry closets waste a fair amount of volume with studs and drywall. A simple remodeling strategy is to substitute a tall cabinet pantry in the same location as an old closet. Trading a 4½-in.-thick wall for a ¾-in. plywood end panel nets inches of extra shelf width. The result is a user-friendly pantry in a compact package that can match the rest of the kitchen cabinets.

A compact walk-in (see p. 59) can be made with an interior footprint of about 4 ft. by 4 ft. and an L-shaped arrangement of shelves on two walls. While the length of the room is variable, the width depends on the shelving arrangement and the walking aisle. I consider 44 in. to be a minimum width, affording a 28-in. aisle and 16-in. shelves on one wall only. A long, narrow room like this will still feel tight. Widening such a pantry allows for more comfortable browsing space, wider shelves, and/or shelves on two parallel walls. Note that a room wider than 8 ft. will likely have wasted floor space in the middle. A typical walk-in pantry might take up 30 sq. ft., at 6 ft. wide by 5 ft. deep. A large walk-in could easily double that area, especially if a client wants room for a counter, a step stool, and a spare refrigerator.

Cabinet Pantry

This type of pantry requires the smallest footprint, but it can still pack a lot of storage. Cabinet pantries can be stock items ordered from national cabinet shops, or they can be custom-built from designers' plans. The author prefers the arrangement shown here: a full-height, cabinet-depth pantry with fully extending drawers below a series of pullouts and stationary shelves. Depending on the width of the pantry, it may have a single door or a pair of doors no wider than 18 in. each.

PLAN VIEW

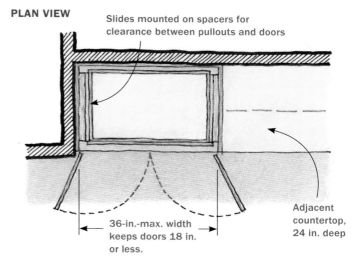

Slides mounted on spacers for clearance between pullouts and doors

36-in.-max. width keeps doors 18 in. or less.

Adjacent countertop, 24 in. deep

ELEVATION

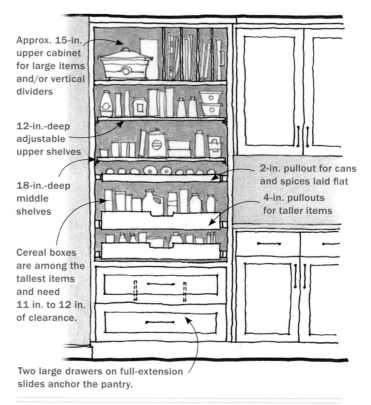

Approx. 15-in. upper cabinet for large items and/or vertical dividers

12-in.-deep adjustable upper shelves

18-in.-deep middle shelves

Cereal boxes are among the tallest items and need 11 in. to 12 in. of clearance.

2-in. pullout for cans and spices laid flat

4-in. pullouts for taller items

Two large drawers on full-extension slides anchor the pantry.

Hard-working doors. Using the back side of a cabinet-pantry door for storage takes away from the potential depth of shelves, but it offers an area where commonly used goods won't get lost in the clutter.

Light you don't have to think about. Good lighting allows you to see clearly. A fixture should be placed inside the pantry or on the ceiling directly outside it. A door-operated switch means you don't have to turn the light on manually or remember to turn it off.

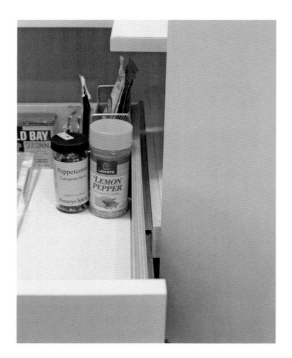

Blocking for clearance. The drawback of sliding shelves behind doors is that the inside of the doors tends to get scratched. The farther you can fur out the shelves from the inside of the cabinet, the better the chance of keeping the doors in good shape.

It's all about storage

While deep shelves can hold more stuff, it's a frustrated cook who can't find the rice hidden behind a train wreck of juice boxes and pasta. For better visibility, I like to stagger the depth of shelves.

A simple pantry with fixed wooden shelving is quick and easy to build. If your budget dictates this approach, consider mounting 16-in.-deep to 18-in.-deep shelves starting about 24 in. above the floor so that you can keep taller items on the floor below. At eye level, switch to 12-in.-deep shelves. Bulkier items on the lower shelves may be taller than 12 in., a common vertical shelf spacing, so allow extra height there—if not all the way across a wall then at least across a portion of it. However, it is common to experience a trial-and-error fitting when first loading a new pantry, so adjustable shelves rate highly on the convenience meter. They also readily accommodate an additional shelf.

For full-height cabinet pantries, I position two big full-extension drawers nearest the floor, enabling items stored in the back to be found easily. Above these drawers, I usually spec a pair of tall doors concealing a combination of pullouts and fixed shelves. This way, users can see the entire pantry at once. I sometimes add a second pair of shorter doors at the top of the cabinet. This space is good for oversize items that are used infrequently. It also can be outfitted with vertical dividers for cookie sheets and the like.

User preferences and heights dictate modifications to my basic cabinet-pantry template. Tall folks may want an additional pullout inside the main compartment. Some like spice racks or small shelves mounted on the inside of the cabinet doors.

Narrow spaces in a base-cabinet arrangement also can be used for pullout pantry units, where the entire assembly extends out from the cabinet frame. Either custom-built or ordered from a catalog, these units have front panels hiding multiple shelves behind, with access gained from both sides when the units slide out. Häfele®, Rev-A-Shelf®, and others sell cabinet-pantry hardware narrow enough to squeeze into a 4-in.-wide space.

Don't forget that wall space inside a walk-in pantry is useful for hanging a mop and brooms, so don't put shelves everywhere.

Give some thought to keeping small appliances in the pantry, plugged in and ready to use. A deep pantry shelf or counter is a possible location for a seldom-used microwave oven. I have a client who keeps a toaster and coffeemaker in her walk-in pantry to reduce the clutter on her counters. Built-in beverage centers take up valuable kitchen real estate. I saved money by putting a freestanding model in our pantry below the staircase.

Doors shouldn't get in the way

While I almost always use standard 24-in.-deep units for cabinet pantries, the width depends on the design specifics of the kitchen. Maintaining a width of 36 in. or less allows me a pair of cabinet doors, each less than 18 in. across. Wider doors can be heavy and unwieldy to open. When I have more than 36 in. of width for a built-in pantry, I place two separate cabinets side-by-side, with three or four doors across the front.

Have you ever had a closet with cheap bifold doors? Used daily, the light-duty hardware gives out; the doors stop gliding and eventually derail. It doesn't have to be so. Outfitted with commercial-grade hardware, bifold door panels are good options for wider reach-in pantry closets. The beauty of these doors is their ability to provide wide openings while being unobtrusive when open. I like to use a pocket door when it is likely to remain open quite a bit or when a swinging door is going to be in the way.

Reach-In Pantry

Enclosed by stud walls, this pantry is a small closet. Reach-in closet pantries tend to be affordable and easy to build. Some have pairs of doors concealing 4 ft. to 7 ft. of shelving across the back wall. Better reach-ins have the widest doors possible for good visibility of the contents. Considering that wide doors take up substantial wall space, this pantry is best located just off the kitchen proper so that the kitchen walls can be loaded with cabinets, appliances, windows, and other essentials.

PLAN VIEW

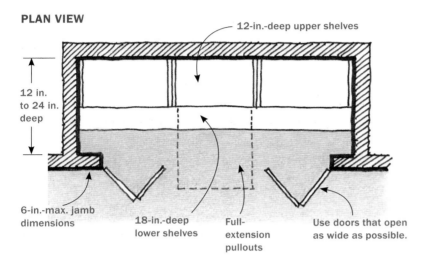

12-in.-deep upper shelves

12 in. to 24 in. deep

6-in.-max. jamb dimensions

18-in.-deep lower shelves

Full-extension pullouts

Use doors that open as wide as possible.

ELEVATION

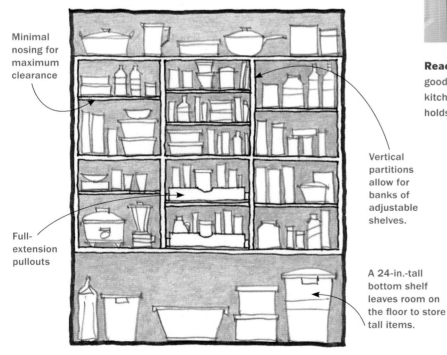

Minimal nosing for maximum clearance

Full-extension pullouts

Vertical partitions allow for banks of adjustable shelves.

A 24-in.-tall bottom shelf leaves room on the floor to store tall items.

Reach in, once in a while. Commonly used goods are stored in the cabinet pantry inside the kitchen. Nearby, this secondary reach-in pantry holds the bulk and is used for restocking.

Walk in to convenience. For a family that buys in bulk, a large walk-in pantry not only hides groceries, but it also offers a place for a second fridge and freezer as well as a beverage cooler.

Walk-In Pantry

Usually the biggest of the lot, a walk-in pantry is ideal for those who buy in bulk and/or live far from the grocery store. Roomy walk-ins are large enough to use three or four walls for storing items such as dry goods, paper towels, pet food, appliances, and brooms. Smaller walk-ins usually have just two walls of shelving. A popular and affordable option for a small walk-in pantry is to put it in a corner of the kitchen, with the door set on a 45° angle between adjoining counters. For those wanting fewer cabinets and an open, minimalistic look in their kitchen, a walk-in pantry just outside the room can be a solution that doesn't compromise the kitchen aesthetic.

PLAN VIEW

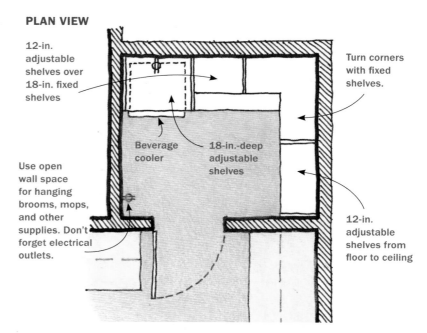

12-in. adjustable shelves over 18-in. fixed shelves

Turn corners with fixed shelves.

Beverage cooler

18-in.-deep adjustable shelves

Use open wall space for hanging brooms, mops, and other supplies. Don't forget electrical outlets.

12-in. adjustable shelves from floor to ceiling

ELEVATION

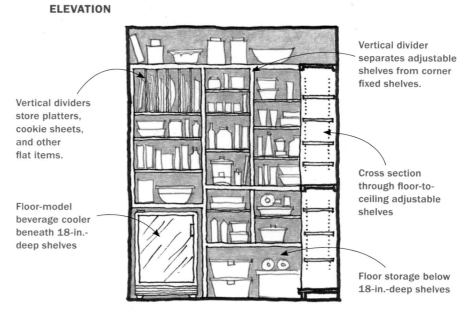

Vertical divider separates adjustable shelves from corner fixed shelves.

Vertical dividers store platters, cookie sheets, and other flat items.

Cross section through floor-to-ceiling adjustable shelves

Floor-model beverage cooler beneath 18-in.-deep shelves

Floor storage below 18-in.-deep shelves

Put it away on the way in. A hybrid pantry/mudroom located between the garage and the kitchen is convenient when you arrive home with groceries and when you are preparing dinner. Counter space near the pantry is always a good idea.

For a single door to a walk-in pantry, I never use less than a 24 in. width, but most folks will appreciate the extra passage of a 30-in. door. You will need a 32-in.-wide door if a big appliance has to get through it, but don't forget that swinging doors take up space. A wide pantry door that opens against a counter will block access. With outswing pantry doors, I keep the doorknob nearest the counter for best functionality. When an outswinger won't work, I fit a pocket door into the blueprint or arrange an inswinger to park against an unused interior wall.

Finally, an automatic light switch that is activated by the door is a nice touch for a pantry because you're likely to be coming or going with your hands full.

Walk-Through Pantry

Sometimes the pantry is part of a mudroom or utility room next to the kitchen. It's often a walk-through room instead of a walk-in. A good example is a pantry/mudroom you pass through from the garage or back porch to the kitchen. This arrangement provides a handy place to wipe your feet and put away items. Storage can be out of view behind doors, or it can be open shelving and bins lining the walls. As a mudroom, it needs space for stowing backpacks, feeding the dog, charging a smart phone, or washing dirty hands. Some might allocate space for an extra freezer or refrigerator.

PLAN VIEW

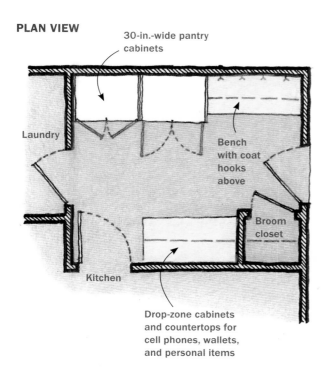

30-in.-wide pantry cabinets

Laundry

Bench with coat hooks above

Broom closet

Kitchen

Drop-zone cabinets and countertops for cell phones, wallets, and personal items

ELEVATION

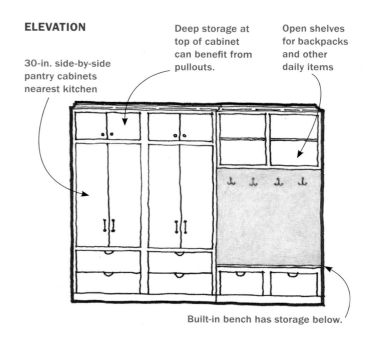

30-in. side-by-side pantry cabinets nearest kitchen

Deep storage at top of cabinet can benefit from pullouts.

Open shelves for backpacks and other daily items

Built-in bench has storage below.

Build a Kitchen Island

RICK GEDNEY

The function of a modern kitchen island can be traced to the familiar kitchen worktable that's been helping families to run the household and prepare meals for generations. An island's job is even tougher, though: A table from the 18th or 19th century didn't need to be a space for making pizza, checking email, or stir-frying. It also didn't have to integrate pipes, ducts, and wires.

I was recently called to a client's house for a full kitchen remodel. The young family wanted to renovate their existing, space-challenged galley kitchen, turning it into a wide-open room with an eat-at island. We looked at the available space and decided a single-level island with a farm sink made the most sense.

One often-overlooked item with island installations is how different floor coverings transition around the cabinets. On this project, we had to make an attractive transition between the wide pine floors in the adjacent living areas and the new kitchen's tile floor. We opted to make the transition at the end of the island and run the wide pine under the eating area. This seemed like the most logical spot to transition between the two types of flooring.

The installation of this island was pretty typical, although the open ceiling in the basement made running pipes and wires to the island a little easier. In this case, the plumber and electrician decided it would be best to do their rough-ins after the cabinets

were installed, although such a process varies from one job to the next. When I'm designing a kitchen island, I always get the general contractor and the subcontractors involved as soon as we have preliminary drawings because plumbing, ventilation, and electrical requirements can make some designs unworkable with a typical budget.

Start with a focal point, then follow the plans

Light fixtures are typically centered over sinks and appliances, so this is a logical starting point for establishing the cabinet layout. From there, move left and right according to the plans, accounting for discrepancies in floor height as you move. With the cabinets aligned, screwed together, and at a consistent height, they can be fastened to the floor.

Center the sink. Using a pair of levels, transfer to the floor the location of the light fixture centered over the sink. This becomes the starting point for the layout.

Work from the end. With the position of the sink's overhead light as a starting point, use the kitchen designer's measured drawings to determine the end of the island. Measure from the wall cabinets to create a parallel line that the island will follow.

Find middle ground. Many installers find the highest point of the floor to reference cabinet height, and then shim up the cabinets that sit on low spots. A better option is to find a cabinet at average height and then shim the low cabinets up and plane the high cabinets down. Shimming and planing should be minimal.

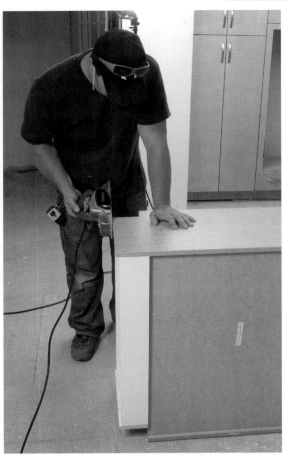

Check across the gap. Where there's a gap in the island's cabinet run for a dishwasher or other appliance, use a long level to ensure that both cabinets are at the same height. Check front and back to confirm that the cabinet tops are in the same plane. Also, make sure that the cabinets are spread the proper distance and that their sides are parallel.

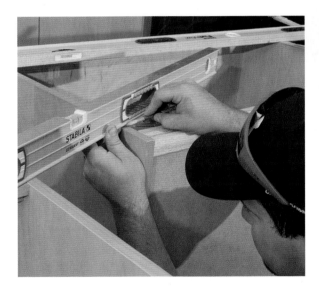

Adjust the height. A few strokes with a power plane quickly remove enough stock to level the cabinet. This planer can remove about $1/32$ in. with each pass while providing a smooth finish. Deeper passes leave a rough surface. Planing should be limited to a maximum of about $3/8$ in.

Lower the high cabinets. Using a level that spans from a high cabinet to one already at the correct height, center the bubble, and adjust your compass scribes so that they reflect the height difference. Use the same tool to mark the base of the cabinet for planing.

Check one more time for inconsistent height. After the cabinet bottom is trimmed, put the cabinet in place and check for level side to side and front to back. If necessary, make further adjustments with shims or planing until the cabinet is level in all directions.

Fasten to the floor. After two or three cabinets are screwed to each other, the cabinets are screwed to the floor. Drill pilot holes at an angle with a $7/32$-in. twist bit, and then use $2\frac{1}{2}$-in. square-drive screws to hold the cabinets to the floor.

Create a seating area

Rather than having extradeep or extrawide boxes, semicustom cabinets often have extended side panels for scribing to walls or other cabinets. These panels often work in conjunction with factory-finished plywood and solid hardwood to cover cabinet backs and empty cavities. The built-in eating area on this island is defined with a plywood panel that matches the cabinets. These additional parts are cut to size before they're fit and fastened.

Trim factory-finished panels on site. Using a track-guided saw, cut a plywood panel to form one side of the island's eating area. Cut it with a 45° bevel to correspond to a bevel on the cabinet's side panel.

Glue mitered joints. The end and back panels meet with a mitered joint. A thick bead of wood glue prevents the mitered joint from opening with changes in humidity. While the glue dries, the joint is held together with 2-in.-wide masking tape.

Blocking reinforces the panel. Use scraps of hardwood or plywood blocking to reinforce the eating area's plywood panels. Pocket screws are a strong, efficient way to make these connections. Previously installed cabinets make a great workbench for drilling pocket holes.

Fasten the blocking. Using 1¼-in. coarse-thread pocket-hole screws, fasten blocking between the top of the plywood and the adjacent cabinet backs. The blocking prevents the plywood panel from warping.

Locate the legs, and cut them to length. A pair of legs support the eating area's overhanging countertop. Use a pair of levels as straightedges to position the legs in plane with the cabinets. Turn each leg upside down over where it will be installed so that it can be marked for trimming on a miter saw. Cut the long part of the leg to keep the top consistent.

Attach the legs to the floor. After drilling a hole in the center of the leg, fasten the leg to a 2½-in. drywall screw (left) that's been cut off with lineman's pliers (above). This anchors the leg in place without visible fasteners.

Install an apron. Secured with pocket screws, a 2-in.-wide apron under the overhanging countertop supports the legs and provides a finished look. A 6-in. apron on the back of the island holds a receptacle.

Add bracing. Two-in.-wide stretchers attach the apron to the back of the cabinets, while angle braces keep the corners square. Both types of bracing are held in place with 1¼-in. coarse-thread pocket screws.

Finishing touches

The finishing touches depend on the individual island, but most islands need drawer and cabinet pulls and some way to hide the obvious seams between cabinets. Appliances and fixtures may be installed now or after the top is in place, depending on the appliances. Once the cabinets are finished, it's time for the fabricator to measure for the countertop.

Hide the seams and screws. The seam at the end of the island where the two cabinets meet is often hidden with a wine rack, bookshelves, or panels. This island has a pair of panels that mimic the cabinet doors. The seam between panels is offset from the cabinet seam, locking the cabinets together. Screws installed from the back side are hidden from view.

Cut the farm-sink opening. Once the cleats that support the sink top are cut and secured to the sides of this cabinet, the installer cuts the blank panel at the front of the cabinet with a jigsaw and cleans it up with a rasp (right). When finished, the sink will be flush with the cabinet.

Time for Templating

With the cabinets in place, the eating area finished, and the farm sink installed, it's time for the stone fabricator to template the countertop. Decisions about thickness, the way the top overhangs the cabinets, and edge treatments should all be decided by this point.

Considerations for Kitchen Islands

RICK GEDNEY

When I first met with the clients whose kitchen is featured in "Build a Kitchen Island" (p. 62), I found a cramped galley kitchen that needed a transformation. Among the clients' requests was a new island where they could cook while keeping an eye on their small children.

Planning an island involves many decisions, but three basic design considerations should be addressed at the start: the necessary clearances, the countertop (single tier or double tier), and the size and type of appliances the island needs to accommodate.

Once my clients and I get beyond these basics, we start working on how the island will look. This conversation often begins with deciding whether the island cabinets should match the other kitchen cabinets. Island cabinets that match the rest of the cabinetry create a unified look, so the island blends into the kitchen. Alternatively, the island's freestanding nature paired with contrasting design elements can make it a focal point for the kitchen. Both approaches can work nicely, but their effects are different.

One of the best ways to shake up an otherwise humdrum kitchen is to pick an island countertop that's different from the surrounding surfaces. The top then can be the star of the show, wowing house guests and inspiring conversation. Concrete, stone, solid surface, metal, and wood all can be used to great effect on kitchen islands. I insist

only that my clients get samples of any likely choices and do their own durability tests with spills and hot pans.

An island's back and sides present another opportunity to introduce a design element. Flush, beaded, or raised panels are all common choices. We also regularly install wine racks, bookshelves, and bulk-storage bins on the sides of kitchen islands. Keep in mind that the base treatment can change the look of an island. A recessed or higher toe space can make an island look free-floating or lend it a furniturelike look, while a baseboard can help to anchor the island in the space.

Critical Clearances

When you're planning an island, the first step should be determining available space and clearances to walls, kitchen appliances, and cabinets. A 48-in.-wide path around the island is ideal, but 42-in. or even 36-in. walkways can work, too, provided that there's enough room to get past open cabinet and appliance doors. Walkways wider than 54 in. require too many steps between work areas. The length of the island depends on what appliances or fixtures will be included. An island with a pro-style range, a farm sink, a dishwasher, or a trash/recycling cabinet requires 78 in. of length alone. If the island is only for food prep, 60 in. may suffice.

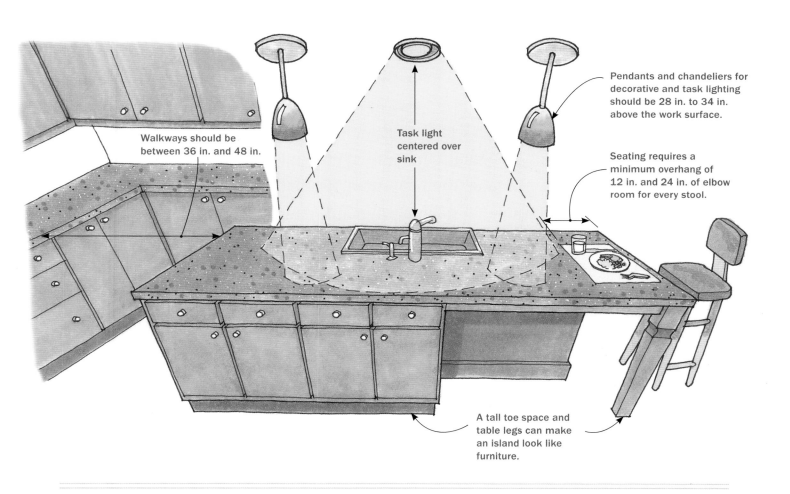

Walkways should be between 36 in. and 48 in.

Task light centered over sink

Pendants and chandeliers for decorative and task lighting should be 28 in. to 34 in. above the work surface.

Seating requires a minimum overhang of 12 in. and 24 in. of elbow room for every stool.

A tall toe space and table legs can make an island look like furniture.

Appliances and Mechanicals

Appliances can add to an island's usefulness. When space is tight, however, choosing the right appliance is important. Door swings should be considered: The doors on dishwashers, for example, vary from 21 in. (the traditional height) to 30 in. (the height increasingly found on high-end models). The choice of appliances surrounding the island is also important. A cabinet-depth, French-door refrigerator may need only 42 in. to accommodate the door swing between itself and the island, while an overdeep single-door model may need 70 in.

For islands with a cooktop or range, ventilation is one of the biggest concerns. Island vent hoods need bigger blowers than wall-mounted hoods because they're pulling air from all sides and are usually installed higher than wall-mounted hoods. As a result, they may need a 12-in. duct. Routing such a large duct can be a problem, however. Many islands use downdraft vents to maintain an unobstructed view, but downdraft vents have their own challenges. They also require large ducts, and some need remote switches that can be tough to locate in a convenient spot.

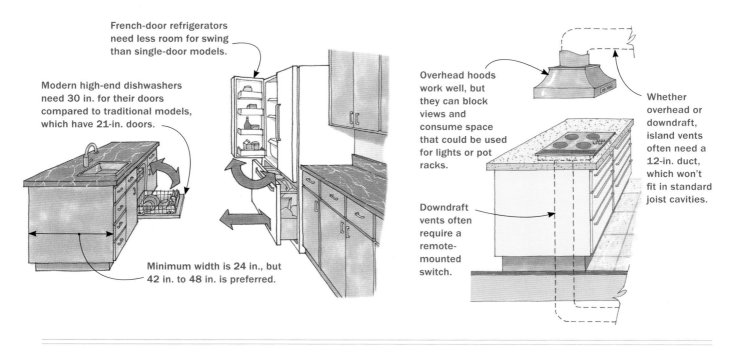

French-door refrigerators need less room for swing than single-door models.

Modern high-end dishwashers need 30 in. for their doors compared to traditional models, which have 21-in. doors.

Minimum width is 24 in., but 42 in. to 48 in. is preferred.

Overhead hoods work well, but they can block views and consume space that could be used for lights or pot racks.

Downdraft vents often require a remote-mounted switch.

Whether overhead or downdraft, island vents often need a 12-in. duct, which won't fit in standard joist cavities.

Two Tiers or One?

Both single- and double-tier islands have advantages and disadvantages. A double-tier island with a raised top between 42 in. and 48 in. can add drama, hide a workspace from an adjacent living area, and break up an otherwise monotonous expanse of countertop. The short section of wall separating the two tiers is also a logical spot for outlets and switches. Double-tier islands generally take up more space, however, because the second tier needs at least an 18-in. countertop to be functional for dining. A single-tier island provides an expansive surface for baking, pizza making, and spreading out a newspaper. Single-tier islands are also less expensive and easier to build.

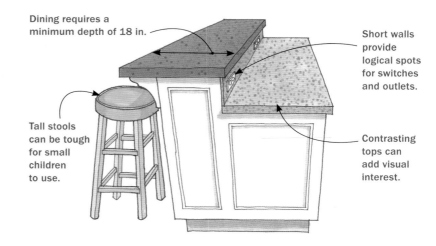

Dining requires a minimum depth of 18 in.

Tall stools can be tough for small children to use.

Short walls provide logical spots for switches and outlets.

Contrasting tops can add visual interest.

Clever Island with Drawers

JOSEPH LANZA

I recently renovated a carriage house that was to be used for entertaining or for extended stays from my clients' family. On the upper level, more than half of the 20-ft. by 24-ft. space was taken up by the kitchen. To make the kitchen efficient, the clients and I wanted the island to be a space for working as well as for gathering and eating.

A few issues came up as I designed the rest of the kitchen. For example, positioning the sink and the major appliances along the outside wall wouldn't leave much space for storage. To have room for seating, the island needed an overhanging counter on three sides, which left room for only two base cabinets. I knew that the big overhang would create space for drawers below the top, a detail seen on many tables. Table-style legs on an island of this size, though, would look bulky and would interfere with seating. My challenge became how to support drawers without legs. Here was my solution: Two plywood base cabinets with solid, substantial tops and backs support a frame of 5/4 poplar glued and screwed together and skinned with a piece of ½-in. birch plywood. This frame supports a countertop of solid 6/4 maple, which, in turn, stiffens and supports the frame. The frame carries the drawers on side-mount slides to save space. The base is covered with 4/4 walnut random-width beadboard, drawers, and door fronts.

Island Top Does Double Duty

To get both seating and storage in this island, the top had to multitask. The key to its success is an open frame made of 5/4 poplar strong enough to support a cantilevered maple countertop, yet with space for six drawers. The addition of a layer of ½-in. plywood creates a structure stronger than the frame alone.

Cut ½-in. elongated holes with a router and a ¼-in. straight bit to allow the top to move seasonally.

Top attached to plywood with 12 #8 by 1¼-in. washer-head screws

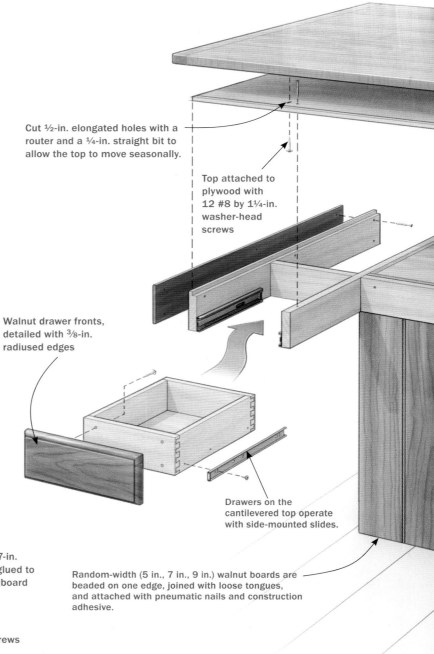

Walnut drawer fronts, detailed with ⅜-in. radiused edges

Drawers on the cantilevered top operate with side-mounted slides.

BREADBOARD END DETAIL

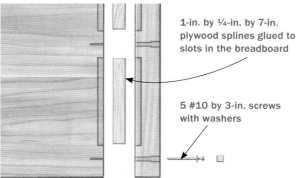

1-in. by ¼-in. by 7-in. plywood splines glued to slots in the breadboard

Random-width (5 in., 7 in., 9 in.) walnut boards are beaded on one edge, joined with loose tongues, and attached with pneumatic nails and construction adhesive.

5 #10 by 3-in. screws with washers

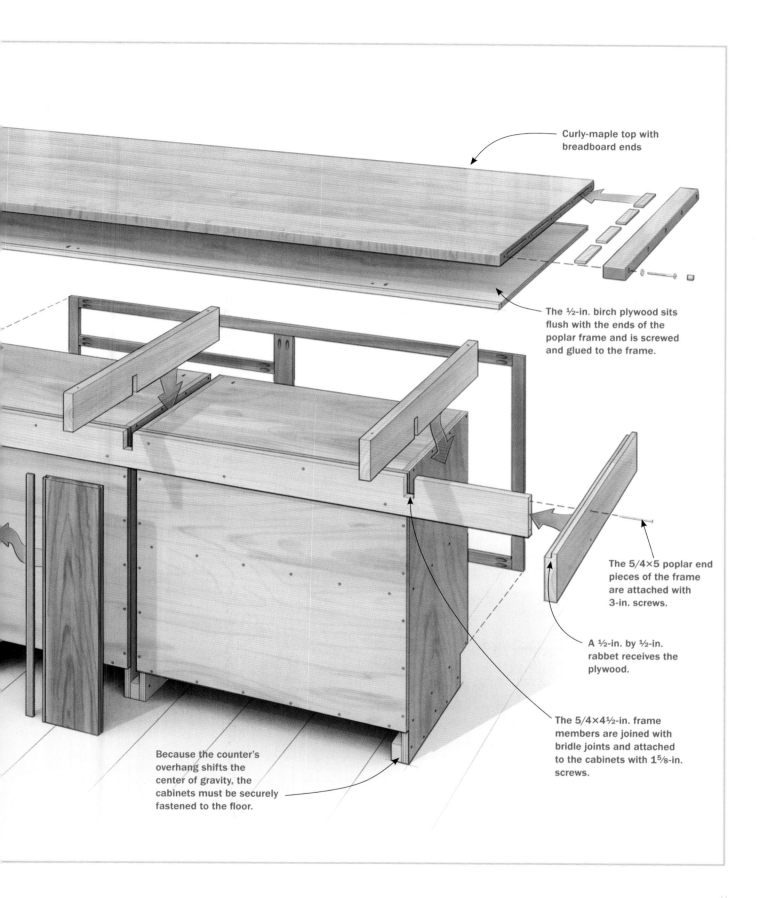

Curly-maple top with breadboard ends

The ½-in. birch plywood sits flush with the ends of the poplar frame and is screwed and glued to the frame.

The 5/4×5 poplar end pieces of the frame are attached with 3-in. screws.

A ½-in. by ½-in. rabbet receives the plywood.

The 5/4×4½-in. frame members are joined with bridle joints and attached to the cabinets with 1⅝-in. screws.

Because the counter's overhang shifts the center of gravity, the cabinets must be securely fastened to the floor.

Start with the boxes

I'm a big fan of simple cabinet boxes, and these boxes fit that category perfectly. I often use ¾-in. birch plywood, and I glue, nail, and screw the butt joints together. I wanted these two cabinets to be able to support the big maple top, so I stiffened them with ¾-in. backs and full (rather than strip) tops. One cabinet holds the microwave, and the other features a drawer above a pair of doors.

At the site, I marked the locations for the boxes and screwed 2× cleats to the floor just inside their footprints at each end. Between where the two cabinets would rest, I anchored another cleat the same thickness as the frame and screwed the cabinets to the cleats.

Integrate the frame with the boxes

To support the top and to house the drawers, I made a frame of 5/4×5 poplar that would extend beyond the cabinets approximately 14 in. To make a more positive connection with the plywood subtop, I cut a ½-in.-deep rabbet along the edge of both end pieces and ripped the remaining pieces down to 4½ in. I cut bridle joints at the appropriate points and attached the frame with glue and screws. I cut the plywood to size, and screwed and glued it to the top of the frame.

Final assembly

Back at the site, I installed the face frames and attached the beadboard. After installing the drawers and their Blum® undermount slides on the work side, I hung the doors and the drawer fronts. On the seating side of the island, I installed the drawers with Accuride®-style side-mount slides. I completed the job by finishing both the walnut base and the maple top with three coats of Ceramithane®, a waterborne urethane.

Check the fit. Because the frame's strength depends on the locations and the tightness of the bridle joints, dry-fit the entire frame around the cabinets before applying glue.

Add the top. Once the frame is assembled, measure and cut a piece of ½-in. plywood that will strengthen the base for the solid maple countertop.

Edges concealed. Although the plywood is hidden by the drawers and trim, the author recessed the plywood into the frame and covered the sides with a band of poplar.

Modular Design Goes Together Fast

Plywood and biscuit construction makes assembly straightforward. Although this design is for a full-size bed, some quick adjustments to the length and width of the parts will allow you to adapt this space-saving design to almost any size bed.

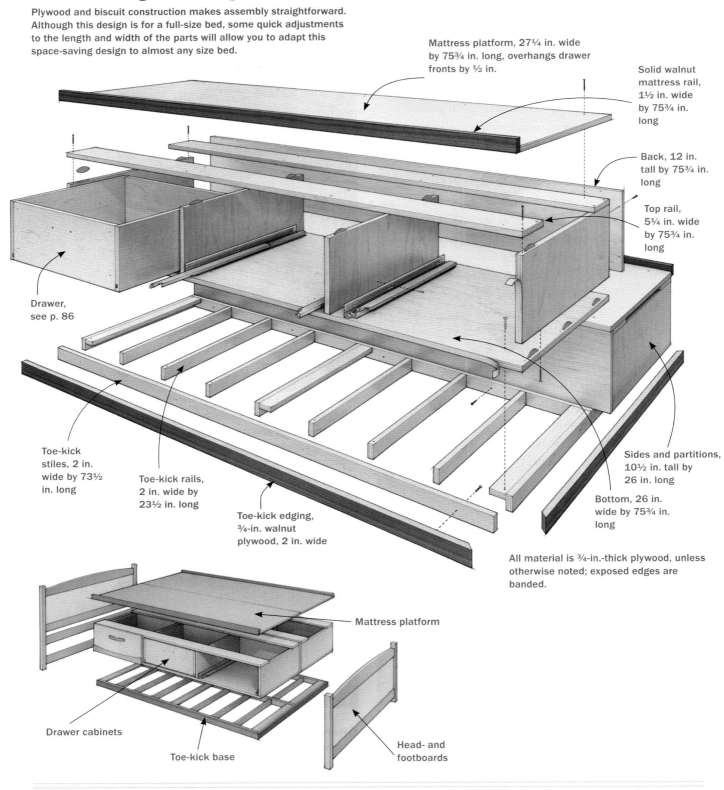

Mattress platform, 27¼ in. wide by 75¾ in. long, overhangs drawer fronts by ½ in.

Solid walnut mattress rail, 1½ in. wide by 75¾ in. long

Back, 12 in. tall by 75¾ in. long

Top rail, 5¼ in. wide by 75¾ in. long

Drawer, see p. 86

Toe-kick stiles, 2 in. wide by 73½ in. long

Toe-kick rails, 2 in. wide by 23½ in. long

Toe-kick edging, ¾-in. walnut plywood, 2 in. wide

Sides and partitions, 10½ in. tall by 26 in. long

Bottom, 26 in. wide by 75¾ in. long

All material is ¾-in.-thick plywood, unless otherwise noted; exposed edges are banded.

Mattress platform

Drawer cabinets

Toe-kick base

Head- and footboards

Biscuits are simple and fast. Biscuit joints make it easy to line up and assemble parts accurately. O'Malley reinforces the joints with screws, which also eliminates the need to clamp these big assemblies. To start, do the ends first. Mark the centers of the middle slots on the face of each piece, and match them up with the center mark on the biscuit joiner (left). No pencil marks are needed for the outer slots (below). Simply align the side of the biscuit joiner with the edge of the work.

Now biscuit the faces. It's faster to clamp the bottom and top rails together to cut the joinery. Clamp a straightedge to the work to ensure that the slots will line up.

Biscuits are simple but rock-solid

After applying the edge-banding, it's time to work on the joinery. Nothing fancy here, just biscuits and screws. The backs get screwed on.

Start by cutting slots for #20 biscuits in the ends of all the vertical parts (sides and partitions); see the photos on p. 83. Next, cut the corresponding slots in the top rails and bottom of each cabinet. To ensure that the partition slots align perfectly, clamp the parts together side by side, and use a tape measure and a straightedge to carefully mark the partition locations on all three parts at once. Clamp a straight piece of wood along your layout lines and use it as a fence as you cut the biscuit slots.

After cutting the slots in the top rails and bottom, drill screw holes at each end of the biscuit slots from the inside (photo at right). To split the glue-up into more manageable steps, I usually glue the biscuits into the top rails and bottom first, then I apply glue to the bottom slots of the vertical pieces and set them in place on the bottom. Next I glue the top slots and set the top rails in place. Tap everything together with a hammer and block, making sure the front edges are flush before the glue sets. Run a countersink bit into the holes that were drilled earlier, and drive 1⅝-in.-long #6 screws into all the holes. Don't forget to put screws into the bottom the same way. Finally, turn the assembled cabinet facedown, position the back, and attach the corners with an air nailer. Then predrill and add screws to permanently secure the back.

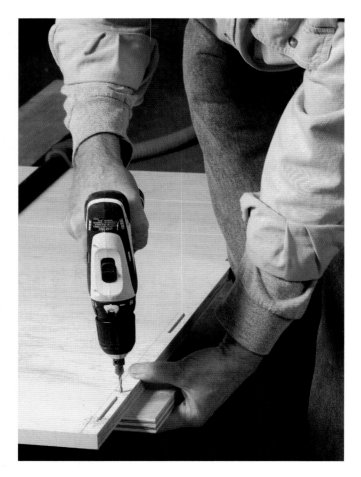

Add the screw holes. Predrilling clearance holes from the inside adds strength and makes assembly easy. A backer block prevents blowout on the outside.

Pre-glue the biscuits. O'Malley first glues the biscuits to the top rails and bottom, breaking the assembly process into more manageable steps.

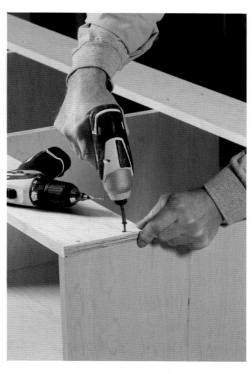

Clamp-free glue-up. Glue the verticals in place, then add the top rails. Make sure everything is flush, then run a countersink in the predrilled holes and drive the screws.

Back goes on last. Once the cabinet is together, position the back, tack it in place with brads, then add the screws.

Use a simple jig to slot the sides. O'Malley uses a shopmade L-shaped jig to hold the sides upright and references off the biscuit joiner's base to cut the slots.

Quick-to-Make Drawers

The plywood drawers are built with biscuits, too. After they are assembled, cut the notches and drill for the commercial slides.

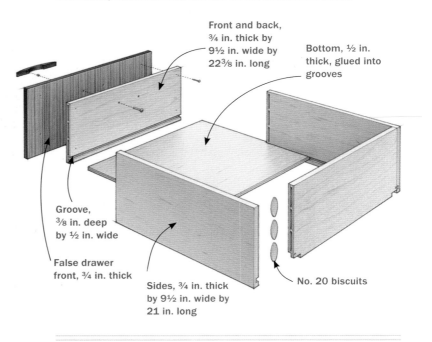

Front and back, ¾ in. thick by 9½ in. wide by 22⅜ in. long

Bottom, ½ in. thick, glued into grooves

Groove, ⅜ in. deep by ½ in. wide

False drawer front, ¾ in. thick

Sides, ¾ in. thick by 9½ in. wide by 21 in. long

No. 20 biscuits

Commercial slides are great for big drawers

For the large drawers, I chose full-extension undermount slides, which are quick to install, are not visible after installation, and give total access to the drawer contents. The slides also are soft closing, which will help keep these big drawers closed and will never slam shut, making them quiet to use.

There are two important details to know when installing these slides. The method for sizing the drawer cabinet is different than for side-mount slides, and the location of the bottom relative to the bottom edge of the sides is critical, so check the hardware instructions before you build the drawers.

Use a tablesaw with a dado blade to cut a groove in the drawer sides for the ½-in.-thick plywood bottoms. Next, put banding on the top edges, cut biscuit slots in the drawer parts, and assemble the drawers. Because the

Make Way for the Slides

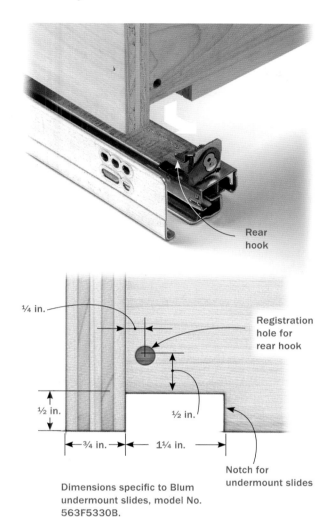

Rear
hook

¼ in.

Registration
hole for
rear hook

½ in.

½ in.

¾ in.

1¼ in.

Notch for
undermount slides

Dimensions specific to Blum
undermount slides, model No.
563F5330B.

Notch the back. To fit the slides, each drawer needs two notches in the back. O'Malley cuts all the notches on one side of the drawers first. Then he moves the fence over to make the remaining cuts.

bottoms are plywood, you can glue them in place. Now use a dado blade to cut two notches in the bottom of the drawer backs for the slides. Follow the hardware instructions for the width of the notches. The dado blade needs to be just high enough to touch the drawer bottom. To be efficient, cut the notches on one side of all the drawers, then reset the fence and cut all the notches on the other side. Now locate and drill the mounting hole for the slide's rear hook and attach

the two drawer-box clips (see the photos, p. 88), following the instructions.

Installing the slides inside the cabinet is easy. Use a combination square to mark the 3/16-in. setback for the front edge of the slides, then screw the slides to the cabinet sides with ⅝-in.-long #6 screws (see the photo, p. 89). Set each drawer onto the slides and slide them back until they engage the mounting clips.

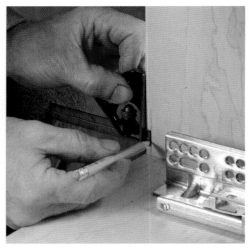

Drill the hole for the slide's rear hook. A simple T-shaped jig helps get the holes in the right spot every time, and works for both sides of the drawer.

Add the base and assemble the bed

With the cabinets and drawers completed, it's time to build the toe-kick base. The base elevates the bed platform off the floor and makes it easy to level the bed if necessary.

Start by clamping the four stiles together and marking centerlines for the rails. Starting with the corners, nail the parts together. Add the flat strips at the ends and middle—these help square up the bases and provide a large surface for screwing the cabinets to the toe kicks. Clamp and screw the halves together. To give it a nice clean look, I added strips of walnut plywood around the sides and end. Position the cabinets flush with the toe-kick at the headboard end and overhanging the toe-kick equally at the sides and footboard. Screw the cabinets together, and then screw the cabinets to the toe-kick (see the bottom left photo, p. 90).

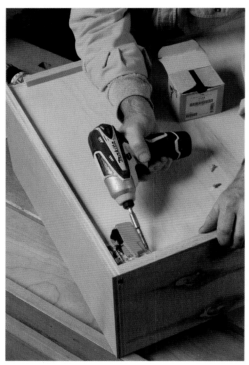

Slides and drawer-box clips. Use a combination square to mark the setback of the slides (top). Attach the drawer-box clips to the bottom of the drawers (above).

Sink the screws. Finish the cabinet assembly by screwing down the drawer slides. Then set the drawers in place.

Next add the two halves of the mattress platform. A solid-wood rail on the edge prevents the mattress from sliding off the platform.

The headboard and footboard are screwed to the ends of the cabinets. Position the headboard carefully, clamp it in place, and connect it using washer-head screws. You can use threaded inserts instead of screws for repeat assembly/disassembly if the bed will be moved often.

When a drawer has a separate, or false, front, mounting it and getting precise reveals can be tricky. The easiest way I've found is to first drill the holes for the drawer handle or knob, and use those holes to position the drawer front. Then, permanently attach it using four holes in the front of the drawer cabinet.

Get the drawer front in place by stacking blocking on the floor under the edges to get the right height, line up the sides, and use a washer-head screw to temporarily attach the front. Carefully open the drawer and drive one of the four mounting screws from inside the cabinet. Close the drawer and make sure it hasn't shifted, and drive the remaining screws. Finally, attach the handles.

Now, plop the mattress down and grab a pillow. You're ready for a good night's rest.

Assemble on site. Get the toe-kick base into position and assemble the bed from the ground up. The modular construction makes it easier to get all the parts in place.

Set the cabinets onto the toe-kick base. Connect them by driving screws through the backs. Make sure they are centered over the base, and then screw them to it.

Attach the headboard. Line up the headboard and attach it with screws from inside the cabinets (top). Then add the mattress platform. Slide the halves into position (above) and screw them down to the cabinets.

Trick for false fronts. Stack blocking under the drawer front to shim into place, and temporarily secure it with a screw through the hardware mounting hole.

Final attachment. Carefully open the drawer and drive a screw in from the back. Check the fit one more time, then sink the other screws.

The final touch. O'Malley connects handmade drawer pulls to complete the bed.

CABINETS

A Cabinetmaker's Kitchen

CHARLES MILLER

For 25 years, Andrew Jacobson has been building museum-quality cabinets and furniture for clients all over the world. From baronial chairs with woven tassels to Art Deco armoires with ebony inlay, Jacobson's company, Petaluma, Calif.-based Design in Wood Inc., has built them all. Jacobson crafts whatever his clients can imagine, no matter how complicated. Turned loose to build his own kitchen, Jacobson looked across the Pacific to the understated elegance and apparent simplicity of Japanese design. It's a timeless aesthetic that puts the emphasis on natural materials—especially wood.

Other than "Aha, I can build a kitchen that demonstrates what our shop can do," there really wasn't a pivotal design goal that unlocked the final plan. Instead, Jacobson and his wife, Peg Schafer, had the luxury of time to work on getting it right. Schafer, an authority on the cultivation of Asian medicinal plants, further strengthened the kitchen's Far East connection.

The predominant cabinet wood is quarter-sawn beeswing sapele, with its ribbony pinstripes arranged vertically, like delicate curtains. The Douglas fir trim, red-elm linen cabinet, jatoba flooring, and walnut-slab countertop were, like the sapele, all acquired from either FSC-certified forests or salvage resources.

The abundant wood, reserved in color and figure, is stopped short of being overwhelming by the other materials in the room. Hand-tooled plaster walls and ceilings bring slight imperfections to the mix. The curvy peninsula countertop, the stainless-steel range hood, and the walnut-slab table soften the rigid grid of the frame-and-panel cabinets. It all adds up to a soothing space to begin and end each day.

A new kitchen combines exemplary woodworking and a practical plan.

A backsplash with just enough drama. A water-washed marble slab inset into a black-granite frame evokes a rippling stream.

Clever solutions. To make room for the recycling and the water filter, a jog in the foundation creates a bump-out at the sink for an extradeep cabinet. To create a linen/dishware cabinet that hugs the wall, a tansu-style hutch looks freestanding but is actually recessed into a cavity in the wall.

Practical details done well. A custom sliding gate with hidden casters in the bottom rail reflects the cabinetry details and keeps the dog out of the kitchen.

Cool detail. A roll-out shelf on heavy-duty drawer slides is clad with a stainless-steel appliance panel, offering a landing pad for hot pots.

Easy to access upper cabinets. Sliding doors open with the pull of a pinky. The door to the appliance garage lifts by way of Blum Aventos hardware.

Galley Style, Entered from the Side

Turn south at the entry, and the view is through the windows over the sink, where the deep counter makes room for generous recycling drawers and a water filter mounted in the back of the sink cabinet.

Design and construction: Andrew Jacobson

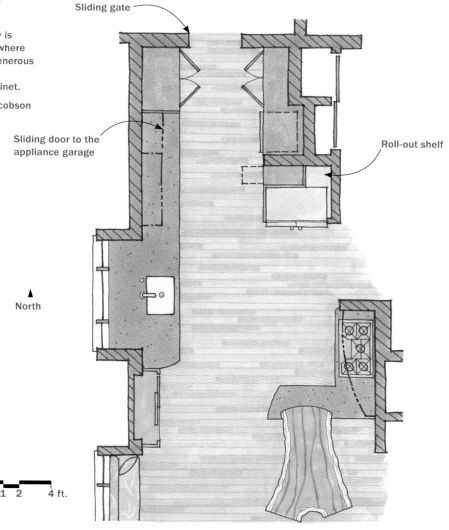

Sliding gate

Sliding door to the appliance garage

Roll-out shelf

North

0 1 2   4 ft.

Sources

Walls and ceilings
St. Astier® hydraulic lime plaster
www.limes.us

Stainless-hood laminate
Chemetal® #727
www.chemetal.com

Counters
Absolute black, diamond-honed granite

Appliance-garage lifts
Blum Aventos
www.blum.com

Tansu pulls
Avigal David
www.tansuhardware.com

Sliding-door tracks
Häfele
www.hafele.com

Simple Hanging Cabinet

CHRISTIAN BECKSVOORT

The Shakers didn't invent the peg board, but they refined it, popularized it, and made it one of their hallmarks. They used peg boards to hang not only hats and clothes but also brooms, mirrors, clocks, chairs, shelves—even cabinets. And their wall-hung cabinets have always interested me. This version was inspired by one of my favorites, a small cabinet from the Hancock, Mass., community. The original had a slab door, but I've substituted a frame-and-panel door. I adapted the semi-circular hanger from a larger cabinet and incorporated half-blind dovetails in the case.

The slight proportions are part of the charm of the piece. The case and the door frame are ½ in. thick, while the back is ⅜ in. and the shelves and door panel are just ¼ in. thick. I've built quite a few of these cabinets, and they look great either painted or clear-finished in pine, cherry, or walnut.

Shaker Wall Cabinet

The cabinet's light but strong dovetailed case is dressed up with non-structural top and bottom panels with overhanging bullnosed edges.

Top, ½ in. thick by 5½ in. wide by 13 in. long

Top rail, ½ in. thick by 1¼ in. wide by 8 in. long

Door panel, ¼ in. thick by 5⅞ in. wide by 11½ in. long

Tenon, ¼ in. thick by 1 in. wide by 1¼ in. long

Face-frame stile, ½ in. thick by 2 in. wide by 14 in. long

Door stile, ½ in. thick by 1¼ in. wide by 14 in. long

Door knob with spinner

Groove, ¼ in. wide by ¼ in. deep, centered

Bottom rail, ½ in. thick by 1¾ in. wide by 8 in. long

Tenon, ¼ in. thick by 1½ in. wide by 1¼ in. long

Screws secure case to top.

Groove, 3/16 in. wide by ¼ in. deep, 5/16 in. from back edge

1-in. butt hinges

Notch, 5½ in. wide by ½ in. deep

Hanger hole, 1 in. dia.

1½ in.

Rabbet, ¼ in. wide by 3/16 in. deep

Case top, ½ in. thick by 4 in. wide by 11¾ in. long

Back, ⅜ in. thick by 11⅜ in. wide by 18 in. long, inset ⅛ in.

Shelf supports, ¼ in. thick by ½ in. wide by 3½ in. long

Side, ½ in. thick by 4½ in. wide by 14 in. long

Case bottom, ½ in. thick by 4 in. wide by 11¾ in. long

Bottom, ½ in. thick by 5½ in. wide by 13 in. long

FRONT VIEW

12 in.

5½ in.

15 in.

13 in.

SIDE VIEW

5 in.

3½ in.

14 in.

18½ in.

5½ in.

Take your pick. The cabinet's simple design sings in a range of clear finished woods—above, cherry on the left and pine on the right. But it also looks great when painted. For the center cabinet, Becksvoort used Federal Blue milk paint from the Old Fashioned Milk Paint Company.

Tails beget pins. After cutting half-blind tails on the case top and bottom, transfer them to the sides. The case parts are flush at the front, but the top and bottom are inset at the rear to accommodate the back.

Cut the grooves. Once the pins are cut, the sides get grooved to accept the back. Two passes on the tablesaw create the 3/16-in.-wide groove.

Case comes together. Knock the case joints together, following up with clamps if necessary. Check to see that it is perfectly square before setting it aside to cure.

Double Roundover

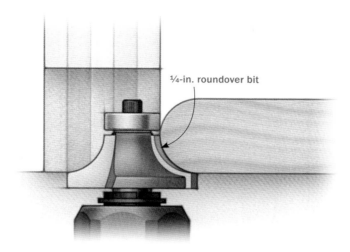

¼-in. roundover bit

Double roundover. The top and bottom get a bullnose profile on three sides. You can gang the two pieces while cutting the roundovers on the router table.

Notch the top. To make the notch in the top for the center section of the back, define the width of the notch with kerfs cut on the tablesaw, then remove the waste between them with the bandsaw.

Pieces of the frame. The pair of stiles that compose a partial face frame are glued to the front of the case without joinery.

Bottom's up. With the roundovers cut and sanded, glue the bottom to the case.

Simple shelf supports. A couple of finishing nails secure the small strips of solid wood that act as shelf supports.

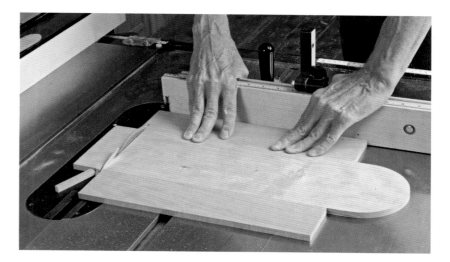

Three-part back. Shape the back's half-round top section before gluing on the two narrower side boards. Then trim the whole back to length and width.

A small, strong case

The original cabinet's case is nailed at the corners, but I made mine with half-blind dovetails for additional strength. Lay out and cut the dovetails using your preferred method, keeping in mind that while the case parts will all be flush at the front, the sides are wider than the case top and bottom because they are grooved for the back.

Before assembly, sand the inside surfaces of all four pieces. Then glue and clamp, checking to be sure the case is perfectly square. When the glue is dry, plane or sand the exterior surfaces flat and smooth.

While the case is curing, make the cabinet top and bottom. With a roundover bit at the router table (see the drawing on p. 101), shape the bullnose on their front and side edges, where they'll overhang the case. Glue the bottom to the case at this point, and then add the face-frame stiles and the shelf supports.

Two tongues. Two passes on the tablesaw—one with the back standing on edge—create the tongues on the sides of the back.

Circle session. A Forstner bit in the drill press cuts a clean hanging hole in the back.

Secure the back. Slide the back into place, then add the top (left). To attach the top, drive screws up through the case top. Then fix the back, screwing it to the case top (above) and case bottom.

Back business

To simplify shaping the half-round hanger, I made the back by gluing up three boards a long, wide center board sandwiched between two narrower, shorter ones (top photo, p. 103). Shape the half-round at the top of the center board at the bandsaw, and refine the curve at the disk sander or by hand. Then glue on the side boards.

Next, use a Forstner bit to drill a 1-in. hole in the center of the half-round. Then trim the back to width, being certain to cut from each side to keep the hole centered. After cutting tongues along the side edges of the back, insert it in its grooves to test the fit. You should have a total of about ⅛ in. of play from side to side to allow for seasonal expansion.

Diminutive frame and panel. After applying finish to the ¼-in.-thick door panel, drop it into place as you assemble the door frame.

Nail the panel. The panel needs to move with the seasons, so it gets no glue. With the bridle joints glued and clamped, drive a brad through the frame and into the panel to keep it centered.

At last, the pull. A simple spinner and a Shaker mushroom knob provide the cabinet with closure.

Light door for a small cabinet

Build the door so that its overall dimensions match those of the opening. That will give you the material you need to make a good final fit. Since the stiles and rails are relatively small, I use bridle joints at the corners instead of the more traditional blind mortise-and-tenon. This gives a larger glue surface and more strength.

When cutting the door panel to size, you can let it bottom out in the grooves in the top and bottom rails, but be sure it has about ⅛ in. of play from side to side for seasonal movement. Glue and clamp the four bridle joints, but don't glue the panel—a brad at the top and bottom is all you need to keep it centered.

When you've glued up the door, trim just enough to produce a ¹⁄₁₆-in. reveal around the top and the sides, and about ³⁄₃₂ in. on the bottom. Use a pair of 1-in. butt hinges to hang the door. Then add a knob and a stop or spinner, apply finish, and you're ready to hang the cabinet on a peg board—or right on the wall if you wish.

Three Types of Curves

The cabinet blends the sawn curves on the case with two different types of laminated curves in the doors and drawer fronts.

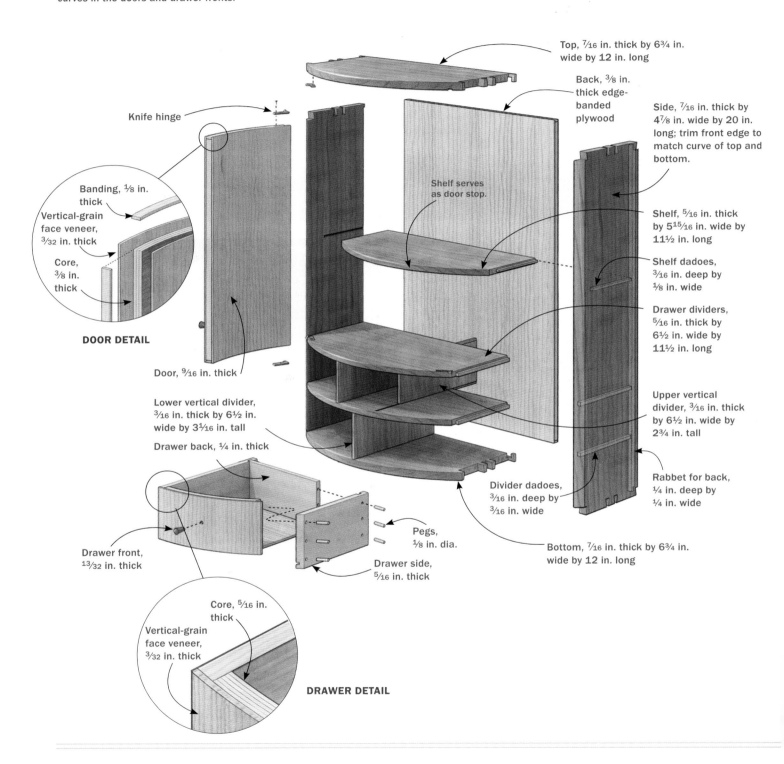

Top, $7/16$ in. thick by $6\frac{3}{4}$ in. wide by 12 in. long

Back, $3/8$ in. thick edge-banded plywood

Side, $7/16$ in. thick by $4\frac{7}{8}$ in. wide by 20 in. long; trim front edge to match curve of top and bottom.

Knife hinge

Banding, $1/8$ in. thick

Vertical-grain face veneer, $3/32$ in. thick

Core, $3/8$ in. thick

DOOR DETAIL

Shelf serves as door stop.

Shelf, $5/16$ in. thick by $5^{15}/16$ in. wide by $11\frac{1}{2}$ in. long

Shelf dadoes, $3/16$ in. deep by $1/8$ in. wide

Door, $9/16$ in. thick

Drawer dividers, $5/16$ in. thick by $6\frac{1}{2}$ in. wide by $11\frac{1}{2}$ in. long

Lower vertical divider, $3/16$ in. thick by $6\frac{1}{2}$ in. wide by $3^{1}/16$ in. tall

Drawer back, $1/4$ in. thick

Upper vertical divider, $3/16$ in. thick by $6\frac{1}{2}$ in. wide by $2\frac{3}{4}$ in. tall

Rabbet for back, $1/4$ in. deep by $1/4$ in. wide

Drawer front, $13/32$ in. thick

Pegs, $1/8$ in. dia.

Divider dadoes, $3/16$ in. deep by $3/16$ in. wide

Drawer side, $5/16$ in. thick

Bottom, $7/16$ in. thick by $6\frac{3}{4}$ in. wide by 12 in. long

Core, $5/16$ in. thick

Vertical-grain face veneer, $3/32$ in. thick

DRAWER DETAIL

FRONT VIEW

12 in.

13¼ in.

20 in.

2½ in.

2¾ in.

2½ in.

SIDE VIEW

6¾ in.

TOP VIEW

12 in.

4½ in.

C/L

Case top, bottom, and
drawer dividers, 9⅛-in.
radius

Shelf, 8³⁄₁₆-in. radius

Sawn curves for the case.
Shopmade templates guide
the shaping of the curved
front edge on the case top,
bottom, dividers, and shelf.

Power of the pivot. Since this is a radius curve, a simple circle-cutting jig lets the router clean up the sawn edge, creating perfectly smooth, consistent arcs on the template.

Attach fences. Complete the routing template by gluing on three fences that partially enclose the workpiece and are sized to hold it in place without clamps. Kenney used cyanoacrylate (super) glue.

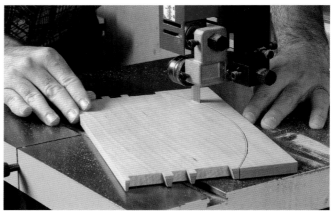

Bandsaw first. After tracing the template's arc onto the workpiece, bandsaw close to the line to rough out the curved edge.

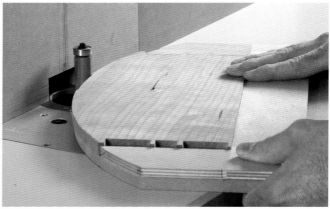

Rout with the template underneath. The bit's lower bearing rides the template surface beneath the workpiece.

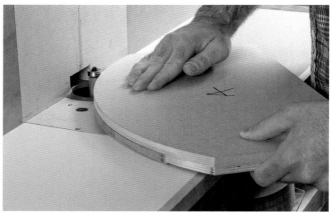

Flip and rout down the other hill. With the workpiece underneath, Kenney lowers the bit so that its upper bearing rides the template.

Template routing creates the curves for the case

When doing curved work, it's easier to cut the joinery while the parts are still square. I started by cutting and fitting the case dovetails and then routing the stopped dadoes for the dividers and shelf. I cut the tails at the bandsaw and routed the pins. Afterward, I turned my attention to the curves. The case has sawn curves on the front edges of its top, bottom, drawer dividers, and shelf. To create a matching curve on each, I made a pair of MDF templates that do two things: First, they provide a measured and perfectly shaped curved edge to which the workpiece can be routed flush. Second, they hold the work securely, from underneath or above, without clamps. I used the templates in conjunction with a flush-trimming bit fitted with bearings both above and below the cutter, so I could flip the template and workpiece to avoid routing against the grain. One of the templates works for the top, bottom, and divider. The other template,

with a smaller radius, is used for the shelf.

To prepare for routing, set each workpiece in the template and trace the curve, then rough out the parts on the bandsaw. Now take the template and workpieces to your router table. Be sure to orient each workpiece in the template in the same way, (i.e., top down) to ensure that the shape is reproduced exactly the same way on each piece.

Because the grain changes direction along most curves, the best way to avoid tearout when routing is to make the cut in two passes—each starting at the top of the curve and traveling "downhill" toward the end of the workpiece. To feed the work into the bit correctly, you'll need to flip the workpiece between passes. This template design makes it easy—there are no clamps to get in the way, and the double-bearing bit works with the template above or below the work. Start with the top and bottom. I made the first pass on all the parts before adjusting the bit to match the flipped template for the second pass.

Continue the curves. Dry-fit the case and mark the sides for beveling (above left). After sawing away the bulk of the waste, plane the edges flush with the front edge of the cabinet (above right).

Leave the dividers proud. After gluing them into their stopped dadoes (above left), use a block plane to trim the front edges flush with the rest of the cabinet front (above right).

Bending ply for the doors. Each door is built on a core formed with multiple layers of thin bending plywood stacked with commercial veneers.

The sides must be beveled to match the curve on the front. Dry-fit the case and mark the bevel, which you can then cut on the tablesaw. Next, rout the shape of the drawer dividers and shelf and cut their tongues. Then rout dadoes in the drawer dividers for the vertical dividers. The design of the knife hinges I used in this case requires that their mortises be cut before glue-up. There just isn't room to do so afterward.

Once these mortises are complete, glue the case together. After it is out of clamps, fit and glue in the drawer dividers. Make the vertical dividers and glue those in, too. Don't glue in the shelf yet.

Bending ply helps the doors take shape

I made the doors using the sturdy bending form shown on p. 113 and following Michael Fortune's method in "Curved Panels Made Easy" (*Fine Woodworking* #210). Each door, at its core, is made from alternating layers of thin, flexible plywood and commercial veneers. Each layer is set with its grain at 90° to its neighbors—a pattern that locks

Glue Up the Core

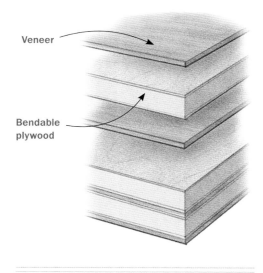

Veneer

Bendable plywood

Strong, Smooth Bending Form

The form is made from ¾-in.-thick MDF ribs and spacers covered with a skin of bendable plywood. The base is glued up first and then the curved cover is clamped with the vacuum bag. Afterward, cover the plywood with packing tape so that glue won't stick to it.

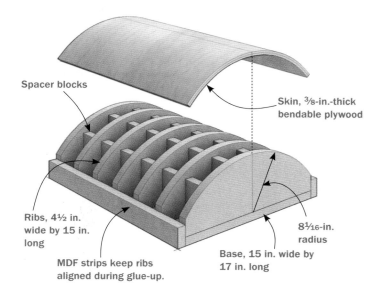

Spacer blocks

Skin, ⅜-in.-thick bendable plywood

Ribs, 4½ in. wide by 15 in. long

MDF strips keep ribs aligned during glue-up.

Base, 15 in. wide by 17 in. long

8¹⁄₁₆-in. radius

Secure the glue-up on the form. Stack the core as shown in the drawing at top left. Small nails driven into the centerline of the glue-up at both ends hold the panel steady while securing it with packing tape.

Into the bag. The form and the glue-up go into the vacuum press. Leave the assembly under pressure for at least six hours.

in the bend when the panel is glued up. This rigid foundation is eventually skinned with beautiful shopsawn veneer.

Start by gluing up an oversize sandwich of inner-core layers, using the vacuum bag to press them into shape on the bending form. Make this panel long and wide enough to yield a pair of doors. I rout the top edge square, then use my tablesaw crosscut sled to cut the panel in two, and rip each door to width, factoring in the thickness of the edge-banding.

After those cuts, attach edge-banding on each door's top and bottom edges with yellow glue. Leave some excess thickness to plane away when fitting the door in its opening, which you should do before gluing on the face veneers. That way you can fix a mistake by gluing on more banding and trying again. With the doors fit top to bottom, glue bandings onto the sides and plane them flush. Now it's time to glue on the face veneers.

I sawed the face veneers from vertical-grain Douglas fir, cutting each veneer about ³⁄₃₂ in. thick and leaving them long enough for the doors and the drawers beneath. The grain runs vertically and flows from the drawers up into the doors. Glue the veneers in place, one face at a time, in the vacuum bag.

Lay out and rout hinge mortises on the doors, then hang them to check the fit. Adjust by planing the inside edge of each door, then rehang and recheck. Repeat until the doors close with a gap between them that matches those on the outside, top, and bottom.

Clean up one edge. With the panel slightly proud of the bending form, a straight bit trims one end square.

Cut It to Size

To rout one end of the panel square, Kenney stands both form and panel upright against his bench, supports them underneath, and straps them in place. He then screws an MDF platform atop the form to support the router.

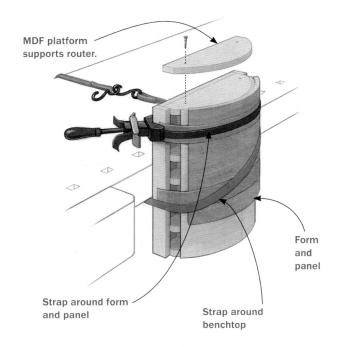

MDF platform supports router.

Strap around form and panel

Strap around benchtop

Form and panel

Rip the panel in half. With the trimmed end against the sled's fence, Kenney centers the panel on the sled's kerf and rips it in half. A loose batten on either side keeps the piece from rocking.

Bandings before veneers. Glue on the solid-stock top and bottom bandings, then trim them flush at the router table (top left). Fit the door to the case vertically, and then add the side bandings (above). The veneers on the front and rear faces (left) are glued up separately in the vacuum bag.

Bent-lams for drawer fronts. Each drawer front is glued up from five plies of shopsawn veneer. The face veneer goes on after the drawer is assembled.

With the doors fit, you can glue in the shelf. Its center should touch the back of the doors (where they meet in the middle) and act as the door stop. Put some glue in the dado and slide in the shelf. Make sure that the doors are flush with the outside of the cabinet when they are resting against the shelf. Clamp across the width of the cabinet to hold the shelf in place until the glue dries.

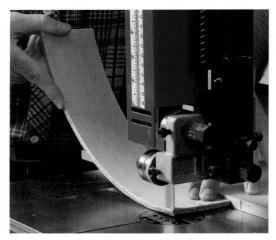

Start at the bandsaw. Resaw the plies for the drawer fronts at 1/16 in. thick (top). Joint the face of the board after each cut. Secure the blank with two nails (center), cover with a caul, and pull the ends down with packing tape. After jointing one edge of the glued-up blank, trim the blank to width at the bandsaw (above).

Final touches. A curved fence at the router table makes it easy to cut the groove for the drawer bottom (top). At the tablesaw, a curved auxiliary fence for the miter gauge holds the workpiece securely and ensures that the end grain is cut at the correct angle (above).

For drawer fronts, bent-lams are a solid proposition

I make the curved drawer fronts from five plies of ⅟₁₆-in.-thick solid stock, laminated and bent to shape in the vacuum press with a layer of face veneer added in a second step. I used the same bending form used to make the doors.

The drawer fronts aren't as thick as the doors, so mathematically they should need a bending form with a slightly larger radius. But laminations from solid stock will "spring back" slightly toward straightness after glue-up. This will leave the fronts very close to matching the curve of the doors. The solid fronts can also be handplaned after assembly (but before the face veneers go on) to remove any remaining variation.

Glue up two separate laminations, one for each bank of drawers. That's because I've found that a blank wide enough to yield both banks tends to warp a little after coming out of the vacuum bag. Leave the laminations in the bag at least four hours (the glue dries more slowly in the bag than it does on a bending form in open air).

Take each blank from the bag, scrape the glue from one edge, and joint that edge. Then run the jointed edge against your bandsaw fence to rip the blank to width. To rout a groove for the drawer bottom in each blank, I used a slot-cutting bit buried in a steeply curved fence on the router table. I used the same setup to groove the straight drawer sides. Another curved fence, this one attached to my tablesaw's miter gauge, was used to cut the drawer fronts from the long blanks for each row. The fence holds the blanks in the correct orientation to the blade so that the end grain is cut at the correct angle. To keep the workpiece oriented properly on the jig's centerline, start with the cuts on the outside before separating the drawers in the center. This ensures that the ends of the drawer front will mate squarely with the drawer's sides.

The assembly is still a little difficult to clamp because the canted orientation of the drawer front makes it want to pivot under clamp pressure. So I used a couple of braces —thin pieces of scrap attached to the drawer sides with double-faced tape—to keep the

Mark the front's location. Working from a full-size drawing, mark the drawer sides for the location of the drawer front.

Attach braces and apply clamping pressure. A couple of pieces of thin stock backed with double-faced tape prevent the drawer front from pivoting as the clamp tightens.

Pegs reinforce the joint. Kenney seats three shopmade pegs in holes drilled on each side, then trims them flush with a pullsaw and chisel.

front from shifting. After gluing up, pegging, and fitting the drawers, slide each one into its opening and mark the front of each side for trimming with a handplane. With the sides trimmed, check that the curve of the drawer front matches that of the case. If it doesn't, trace the cabinet onto the front and plane the front down to the line.

To ensure that the grain flows nicely from the drawers to the doors, you must take out the full width of the vertical dividers when cutting the drawer front veneers to length. Otherwise, all those nice growth ring lines won't line up. Glue on the veneers using curved cauls and plane them flush to the drawer front. For the end grain, which is on the top and bottom of the drawer, work in from both sides so that you don't tear it out. Finish the drawer construction by cutting, rabbeting, and installing the drawer bottoms. I secured the bottom with just a touch of glue in the front rabbet.

Attach the face veneer. Painter's tape holds the veneer in place (top left) until the glue-up is secured with clamps and shaped cauls (left). Thin packing foam helps distribute the pressure.

Install the bottom. The curve on the bottom's front edge is cut at the bandsaw after tracing the profile from the glued-up drawer.

Semicustom, full of options. Semicustom lines offer so many standard options that most of us don't need a custom shop to find what we're looking for. Face framed, frameless, or both? You don't have to choose. These cabinets from Canyon Creek offer a clean, frameless look with face frames hidden behind the door and drawer fronts. Some installers prefer this arrangement for durability and ease of installation.

space. Standard cabinet depths and heights also can be increased or decreased for an upcharge. So if using a standard 24-in.-deep base cabinet doesn't allow adequate clearance in a pantry or a passageway, you can reduce the box depth and still use the particular cabinets you were hoping for. Standard wall cabinets are 30 in. and 36 in. tall, but sometimes 33 in. or even 42 in. works better with a particular ceiling height. Again, with most semicustom lines, this level of customization is possible.

Semicustom cabinets are available with face-frame or frameless construction or both. The choice is mostly aesthetic: Face frames are more common on traditional-style cabinets, and frameless cabinets are more contemporary looking. But there are plenty of exceptions.

On face-frame cabinets, the doors can be inset or they can be overlaid to reveal more or less of the frames. The hinges attach to the face frames. Doors on frameless cabinets cover the cabinet box's finished front edge.

Pullout pantry is narrow enough. Standard cabinet widths start at 9 in. and can be specified in 3-in. increments (or smaller for an upcharge). This pullout spice rack from Merillat is a great use of narrow space next to the oven and cooktop.

No wasted space. This clever end-panel door from MasterBrand makes the most of a few unused inches for magazine storage and office supplies.

Door hinges attach to the box sides. Frameless construction offers a more open interior and is typical of today's European cabinetry. In the United States, by contrast, face-frame construction outsells frameless, according to Danielle Mikesell, Merillat's director of marketing. Both traditional and frameless cabinets can be ordered with a panoply of door and drawer styles, wood species, finishes, crown-molding profiles, and box-construction options. Some manufacturers will even combine face-frame construction with a frameless aesthetic. When it comes to style and construction, most of what is commonly built by custom-cabinet shops can be found in semicustom cabinets.

Cabinet doors and shelves are typically ¾ in. thick. A loaded, ¾-in. shelf can span a 36-in.-wide cabinet, while thinner shelves may bow across that span. Full-depth shelves, adjustable in ½-in. increments, maximize storage. For organizing cabinet interiors, there are plenty of accessories, such as roll-out shelves and lazy Susans. Companies such as Häfele, Knape & Vogt®, and Rev-A-Shelf® make bins, baskets, and recycling containers to complement semicustom lines.

Semicustom lines offer warranties that may equal the limited-lifetime warranty typical for custom cabinets. Canyon Creek, Merillat, and KraftMaid® all offer such warranties on some lines that cover the product for as long as the purchaser owns it, with certain exclusions. Unfinished products are excluded, for example, as are normal wear and tear, instances of abuse, and improper installation. Merillat's Classic, also a semicustom line, has a 25-year warranty.

Hardware matters. Most manufacturers offer hardware options to enhance storage in their cabinets. Some can be outfitted with aftermarket hardware as well. These Diamond cabinets have elegant and useful storage that keeps cookware from getting lost deep inside the island.

We can't tell you what it will cost

It would be great to read an article or visit a website and get a firm figure for what your cabinets might cost, but it's not that simple. Calculators can give you a range, but the offerings of semicustom cabinetmakers are vast, and even some seemingly logical questions—such as whether face-frame or frameless cabinetry is more expensive—are not so easy to answer.

Let's explore that example: Frameless boxes ought to be ¾ in. thick to provide good purchase for door hardware, whereas a face-frame box can be ⅝ in., because door hardware is not attached to the box. So frameless cabinets, in general, must be more expensive. But without face frames, those

European-styled cabinets don't use as much hardwood or require as much labor. So it seems that traditional cabinets must be more expensive. But filler strips can mar the clean lines of modern, frameless cabinets, so you'll want to specify custom box dimensions, increasing the cost. You still haven't specified a door and drawer style, a finish, or all the storage upgrades you want.

In short, distinguishing by frameless or traditional construction, dovetail or dowel joinery, or one particular feature or finish is not a meaningful way to compare prices. For every instance where one company's product costs more, there are others where you will find the opposite. Showrooms offering semicustom lines have a list of "retail" prices for every component in a cabinetry manufacturer's line. What the showroom charges a customer, however, depends first on its discount calculation—a percentage assigned by the manufacturer—and then on how it adjusts that discount to cover its cost of business. The discount calculation varies based on the dollar volume of that cabinetry line sold by that showroom, among other factors.

The purchaser's price for a kitchen with dozens of components might include up-charges for customized dimensions, premium wood species, certain finishes and hardware,

Why so many lines? MasterBrand Cabinets alone has nine cabinet lines ranging from stock to custom. It's semicustom lines include Homecrest®, Schrock®, Kemper®, Kitchen Craft, Diamond, and Decorá. According to Stephanie Pierce, MasterBrand's design studio manager, each brand is tailored to a slightly different customer. MasterBrand's Diamond line, shown here, is designed and marketed toward busy homeowners who value flexibility and function.

or glass doors (which require a finished cabinet interior). How badly a showroom wants the business can also affect price comparisons between showrooms. With so many factors influencing the final price, you'll have to talk to a designer or dealer to get a legitimate estimate.

For style. MasterBrand's Decorá line, shown here and above, is meant for style-savvy homeowners who want lots of options for personalizing their kitchens.

Four Ways to Assess Quality

Experts agree on what distinguishes a quality semicustom cabinet: box construction, drawers, doors, and finish. In addition, hardware—drawer slides and door hinges—should be well-made and adjustable. Blum, Grass®, and Häfele are examples of top-quality hardware brands.

Boxes

Today's semicustom cabinet boxes can be made from plywood, particleboard, or medium-density fiberboard (MDF). Even if different boxes meet the same testing requirements and have equal warranties, there are variations to note in the materials used.

To begin with, not all plywood is created equal. There are different grades, and the number of plies can vary. Assuming high-quality glue and fabrication methods are used, the more plies a panel has, the more stable the panel will be. Plywood is typically the most expensive option for cabinet boxes.

Another option, formaldehyde-free particleboard (sometimes called furniture board) is not the cheap, porous particleboard of the past. It is a dense and durable substrate for veneer and is often more affordable than plywood cabinet boxes. It can be sized and cut with great precision, as can MDF.

MDF is made from recycled wood fibers and resin. As the smoothest of the three box materials, it is an excellent substrate for both veneer and paint. MDF's downside is its heaviness.

Drawers

You're likely to find dovetailed and doweled drawer construction in most semicustom cabinet lines. Both are equally sturdy, though dovetails add character and a high-quality appearance. You won't likely find glued or stapled drawers in semicustom cabinets. If you do, consider upgrading. Dovetails and dowels not only look better, but they last longer.

For a durable drawer, the hardwood or MDF fronts should be applied to a four-sided drawer box, not used as the fourth box side. Drawer boxes typically have ½-in.- or ¾-in.-thick solid-wood sides, although Canyon Creek's semicustom lines feature a ½-in.-thick plywood drawer box. A drawer bottom of 3⁄16-in.-thick plywood resists deflection even when fully loaded. Some semicustom European lines offer metal drawer boxes; a different look, it's perhaps the most durable option available.

When it comes to drawer hardware, full-extension slides separate semicustom cabinets from most stock offerings and provide full access to the contents of a drawer. Undermount slides support the drawer from the bottom; their concealment is aesthetically preferable to side-mounted slides, particularly with dovetailed drawers. A soft-close feature, available on many semicustom cabinets, means they'll close quietly and without slam damage. Avoid drawers that shake or rattle when you operate them, which is a sign of cheap drawer slides.

Doors

Doors don't express a cabinet's overall quality as reliably as the other three items. Even lesser-quality cabinets may have reasonably well-built doors. In any event, look for ¾-in.-thick doors made of hardwood, painted or veneered MDF, or veneered particleboard. Good particleboard is dense (Merillat Classic doors call for 48-lb. particleboard). All doors should have rubber bumpers to cushion their closing action and adjustable hinges from a reputable manufacturer.

Most doors consist of a four-piece frame plus a center panel. A center panel needs room to move in response to humidity, but that doesn't mean it should rattle around in

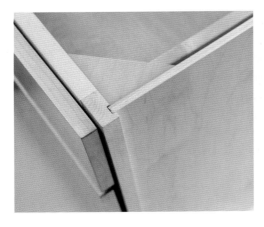

Boxes. A box's quality is determined by the quality of the material used.

Drawers. Look for dovetailed or doweled drawers, which are studier than drawers that are stapled.

Doors. Doors aren't as clear an indicator of quality as boxes and drawers, but they should be high quality with good hardware.

Finish. Between stains and paints and finishing options such as glazing, distressing, burnishing, and antiquing, your choices are nearly endless! Look for a finish that is clear, not cloudy, and drip free.

the frame. A center panel may be hardwood or veneer, but its grain and color should closely match the frame. High-quality doors have a raised center panel set into the door frame facing either outward (a raised-panel door) or inward (a recessed flat-panel door). Raised panels—whether facing in or out—possess a thickness and solidity that distinguishes them from a ¼-in.-thick, flat center panel. Because they do not respond to changes in humidity, MDF doors in a raised-panel style are made of a single piece of material.

Door-edge, frame, and raised-panel profiles can be varied to individualize a semicustom door style, though not every style will be available for both framed and frameless cabinets. There are also laminate and thermofoil door options, but they are more commonly found in stock cabinetry.

Finish

Finish choices vary as much as door styles. Canyon Creek, for example, offers nearly 40 standard stain and paint colors on more than 10 wood species. Glazing, distressing, burnishing, and antiquing add subtle finish variations. Canyon Creek will also mix a finish color to match a paint-store chip.

Stain finishes comprise several steps, usually including stain application, heat curing, one or more sealer coats, and a topcoat. Cabinets are sanded by machine and by hand prior to staining, then sanded again between sealer coats. Companies typically cure stains, sealers, and topcoats with convection heat. The resulting baked-on finish is durable enough to support extended warranties. Bertch® Cabinetry uses a blend of alkyd, amino, and vinyl resins in its sealers; the topcoats are alkyd and amino resins formulated into catalyzed conversion varnish. Sheen levels can be modulated from matte to glossy by varying the topcoat formulation, but all sheens should be equally durable.

"Painted" finishes are achieved using colored (opaque) catalyzed conversion varnishes. These dry harder than standard paint. Even when a semicustom manufacturer matches, say, a Benjamin Moore® color, the resulting paint differs from what's available in retail because the cabinetry formulation must be sprayable and yield more sheen. The paint typically is applied as a primer coat topped with one or more additional coats, with sanding and heat-curing in between. Not all painted finishes receive a separately formulated topcoat as stain finishes do.

A painted finish must be applied to a smooth surface, so paint-grade maple is often used. Because this finish sits on the wood surface instead of moving into the wood like a stain, a painted finish can crack when the wood under it moves. Hairline cracks appear at door and face-frame joints, and are not considered defects. However, the finish should not peel or flake. Most manufacturers offer matching paint for touch-ups along with a cabinet order.

To assess a finish, you need to see actual product samples. The finish should be clear; a cloudy appearance is a sign of poor quality. It should be smooth and drip-free, without visible sanding marks. Molding and door edges should be crisp, with no finish buildup. Low- or no-VOC formulations are desirable.

What's Not Semicustom

The distinction between stock, semicustom, and custom cabinets can be blurry. Some manufacturers, like Merillat, offer lines in more than one category. Here's a look at the alternatives to semicustom.

STOCK refers to cabinet inventory stocked—and sometimes stacked—at a manufacturer or retailer. Options for door style, wood species, finish, molding profile, and hardware are limited to what's there. Materials reflect a budget price point; for example, a stock cabinet door may be ½ in. thick, while a semicustom or custom door measures ¾ in. Cabinet-box size is limited to 3-in.-wide increments from 9 in. to 45 in. Depths for both wall and base cabinets are fixed, and warranties are the shortest on the market—often five years or less. Benefits of stock cabinetry include its entry-level price and fast (immediate or within a few days) delivery. Stock quality may suit a rental unit, starter house, or budget kitchen. Limited choices may inspire DIY creativity and yield excellent value.

CUSTOM cabinets, originating in a small shop or a large manufacturing facility, are built to client specifications upon receipt of the order. They can incorporate curved doors, complex angles, odd box sizes, and unusual colors. If you want to hand-select or book-match exotic veneers, you can. Options for door style, wood species, finish, crown-molding profile, box selection, accessories, and hardware are enormous. Benefits of custom cabinetry include vast choice, tailored fit and finish, and individualized fabrication. Expect a premium price tag and longer remodel time, since custom lead times run eight weeks to several months. Large manufacturers offer generous (even lifetime) warranties for custom products. Small-shop warranties vary. Custom implies top quality, but it's not a given from every small cabinet shop.

Find it

There are far too many semicustom cabinet manufacturers to list. Here are a few to get you pointed in the right direction. To dig deeper, go to a local kitchen showroom or visit the Kitchen Cabinet Manufacturers Association website (www.kcma.org).

Canyon Creek Cabinet Company
www.canyoncreek.com

KraftMaid
www.kraftmaid.com

MasterBrand
www.masterbrand.com

Merillat
www.merillat.com

Installing Semicustom Cabinets

ISAAK MESTER

On the face of it, installing semi-custom kitchen cabinets is pretty straightforward: Attach a run of boxes to the wall, make sure all the doors and drawers work, and don't scratch the paint. Unless kitchens are a regular part of your work week, however, you'll find that the installation can go sideways in a hurry if you don't pay attention to some key aspects of the job. In demonstrating the installation of this fairly typical kitchen, I illustrate the most important tricks of the trade that help to make this a professional-looking job.

First, unpack carefully

The designer and the client picked semicustom cabinets from KraftMaid for the kitchen. In price and quality, they usually represent a comfortable midpoint between small-shop custom cabinets and big-box-store economy cabinets. The carcases are made of plywood, and the face frames, doors, and drawers are hardwood. The quality of the finishes is excellent. The cabinets were configured with a mix of drawer and door bases, two lazy-Susan corners, and some glass-door uppers. Cabinets like these are usually shipped to the job site. The first thing I do is check the shipping manifest against the items shipped, and note any damaged or missing boxes. The faster you start the return process, the faster you'll be able to finish the job.

When taking cabinets out of the boxes, use a knife only when necessary, and don't cut the box along the cabinet's face or you may scratch the finish. Inspect each cabinet to make sure there are no dings, and arrange the return of any damaged units.

Factory cabinets are manufactured in part with hot-melt glue, which tends to dry in heavy drips that can get in the way of an installation. Before installing a cabinet, scrape off any of these drips.

Measure and mark for level

A level run of cabinets starts from a reference point taken off the high spot on the floor or, when there are soffits, the low spot on the ceiling. It's especially important for the base cabinets to be level and flat so that they can adequately support long runs of countertop.

On this job, the kitchen's cathedral ceiling meant that there were no constraints to the upper cabinets, so we based our measurements on the floor. Using a 6-ft. level, I checked the floor along the base of the wall and found a high spot in the corner. Carried out on a level line, this would translate to a gap of more than an inch at the end of the cabinet run—too high to hide with a kick plate or shoe molding.

Start off organized. The best way to start an installation is to make sure that the space is clean and that your tools and materials are right where you need them. After unpacking the first run of cabinets, place them in the general vicinity of their future locations, leaving yourself enough space to work comfortably. Before installing a cabinet, remove its drawers and doors, set them aside, and replace them when the cabinet is set.

Use caution. When opening the cabinet boxes with a knife, steer clear of the face of the cabinet. Don't get excited and learn this simple tip the hard way.

Safeguard the finish. Painter's tape on one edge of a level protects the cabinet finish. When the tape gets dirty, though, it's not helping any longer. Change it often.

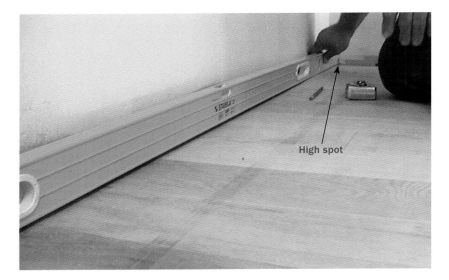

High spot

Establish a reference line. Start a cabinet installation by finding the floor's high spot from which to create a level reference line on the wall to represent the cabinet tops. Use a 6-ft. level to find the highest point in the floor. Extend a level line outward to determine how much the adjacent cabinets will have to be shimmed. If the gap at the end of the run is too large to mask with trim, you'll need to adjust.

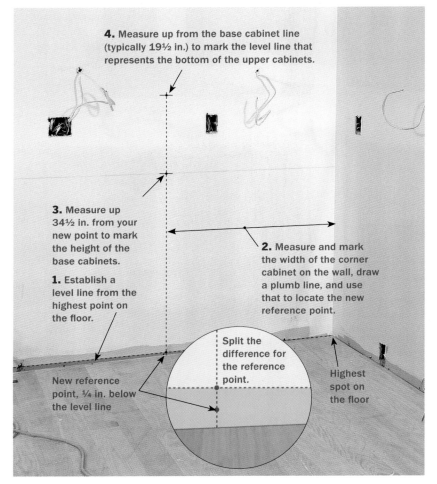

4. Measure up from the base cabinet line (typically 19½ in.) to mark the level line that represents the bottom of the upper cabinets.

3. Measure up 34½ in. from your new point to mark the height of the base cabinets.

1. Establish a level line from the highest point on the floor.

2. Measure and mark the width of the corner cabinet on the wall, draw a plumb line, and use that to locate the new reference point.

Split the difference for the reference point.

New reference point, ¼ in. below the level line

Highest spot on the floor

If the high spot is too high, split the difference. Mark a new reference point below the first line. Measure up 34½ in. to mark the top of the base cabinets.

To avoid this gap, I moved my reference point to the end of the corner cabinet, where my original level line cleared the floor by about ½ in. I then marked a new reference point ¼ in. below the original line. From this new point, I measured up 34½ in. to establish the height of the base cabinets and drew a level line there. I then made another mark 19½ in. above that line to mark the bottom of the upper cabinets, drawing that line out level as well (photo left). When installing the cabinets, I scribed and cut the bases where the floor was higher than my reference mark, and shimmed the bases where the floor was lower.

Start off right. Spend the time to get the first cabinet perfect, and it'll be much easier to install the rest.

Trick of the trade. Align shims with the wall framing so that the mounting screws lock the shims into place.

1

3

2

Many installations start in the corner, so that cabinet must be plumb, level, and square. Here, I had to cut down the corner cabinet to compensate for a high spot in the kitchen's inside corner. To make an accurate cut, I scribed the side panels (1), cut them down with a jigsaw (2), and transferred those cuts to the interior base supports (3). A couple of strategically placed shims brought the cabinet into level compliance.

Compensating for corners

Once you've understood the state of the floor, you have to scope out the walls. It's a rare event when a kitchen's walls are plumb and square. I checked to see that the corner itself was relatively square so that the end cabinet on either side wouldn't flare out from the wall. Corners are often less than square because of the buildup of tape and compound. Sometimes the best solution is to cut or scrape out the compound behind the cabinet to square up the corner.

I like to join the corner cabinet to the adjoining cabinets before attaching them to the wall so that I can carry the corner outward in two directions. If the corner isn't square, I can adjust the cabinet's angles so that there's an equal gap behind the end cabinets, which I usually conceal with a finished end panel. Here, because the line of cabinets was interrupted by appliances, I had the option of adjusting the position of the cabinets independently, but I always try to keep the counter overhang as consistent as possible.

There are times when joining your upper cabinets together on the ground will make the installation much easier and straighter. This is especially true with frameless cabinets, as there is absolutely no play in the installation. Some installers like to hang the upper cabinets first because they don't have to reach up and over the base cabinets. Many kitchen designs (like this one) are driven by appliance locations, though, so it's important to establish the base location first.

When it came to installing the upper cabinets, the first thing I did was to screw a length of scrap brick molding to the wall studs along the upper level line. This serves two purposes: First, it's a third hand to support the cabinets as they're installed; second,

it makes a handy reference when locating screws inside the cabinet. If the area between the bases and the uppers isn't meant to be covered by a backsplash, it's easy enough to patch the screw holes in the walls.

Set cabinets carefully. As you work outward from the first cabinet, it's important to keep the successive cabinets level and in line with the walls. When shimming the front of a cabinet, keep one finger on the top of the face frame of the adjoining cabinet to avoid having to look to see when the two cabinets are even.

Use the right tool. Use a small flat bar as a lever to gain more adjustment control when shimming a cabinet. A multitool does a clean and fast job of trimming shims without disturbing or splitting them.

Set upper cabinets with a ledger. As with the lower cabinets, the upper-cabinet installation begins in the corner and works outward. Secondary support, such as a ledger or cabinet jack, helps to stabilize a cabinet's position while stud and wiring locations are marked and pilot holes drilled.

Use padded bar clamps. To attach the next cabinet in line with the first, making sure to align the face frames. Always countersink a pilot hole for screws, and use decking or similar heavy-duty screws to attach cabinets to each other and washer-head screws to attach cabinets to the wall. Drywall screws are too brittle and shouldn't be used.

Screw a temporary ledger, such as a scrap piece of brick molding, to studs in the wall to help support the upper cabinets. When screwing a cabinet to the wall, transfer the locations of the ledger screws to the inside of the cabinet.

Move the wires to where they belong. Here, the undercabinet feeds should be above the cabinet bottom. On this job, a full backsplash will conceal the drywall repair.

Keep plumbing and electrical neat

One of the details that adds to a good installation is careful integration of cable and pipes in the cabinets. I have encountered too many kitchens where the installers simply hacked out a square in the cabinet back for the water and waste lines, which is visible whenever the cabinet is open.

The first step I take to ensure this integration is to insist that the plumber leave everything stubbed out and capped. It makes it easier to do a careful layout, which in turn makes a neater installation.

Second, I find out what kind of under-cabinet lighting is going to be installed later so that I can drill the holes in the proper locations of the cabinet. There's nothing worse than seeing the lights installed with 2 ft. of exposed wire running across the bottom of the cabinet to the hole that I drilled.

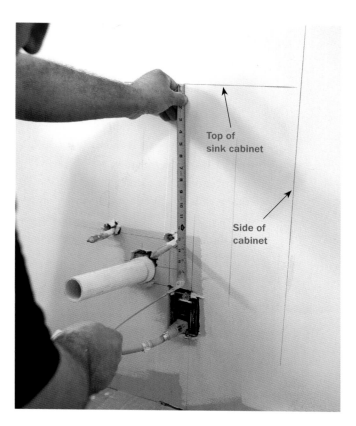

Establish the reference. Find the centerline of the cabinet on the wall, then measure and mark the locations of the cabinet's side and top. Use only these two points to measure the plumbing and electrical locations.

Transfer to the cabinet. From the same two points, measure and mark the centers of the plumbing stubs and the outlet.

¼-in. pilot hole

Drilling for appearances. Drill ¼-in. pilot holes on the center marks from the cabinet back, then drill from the cabinet interior with a sharp hole saw, using its pilot bit as a guide, to minimize visible tearout.

Scribing shouldn't be difficult

Once the cabinets are in, the next step is to scribe and attach the finished end panels. Base moldings, often part of the trim package in semicustom cabinets, cover any gaps between the panels and the floor, so the wall is the critical area to be scribed. After measuring the space and determining the correct width or length of the panel, I shim or clamp the panel's tops equal to the top of the cabinet. Setting a compass to the distance of the largest portion of the gap between the wall and the panel, I scribe the wall's line onto the panel, check the measurement to make sure it's right, and cut away the waste. Full-length panels should be shimmed plumb before they're scribed.

Tips for installing trim

The trim for semicustom cabinets is usually made from prefinished hardwood, and it's relatively expensive and difficult to replace once you've started. Make sure you have enough before you sign off on the delivery, although distributors often can send missing pieces within a few days. Because it's prefinished, the trim must be cut carefully to avoid tearout. Keep nail holes small so they can be concealed with a color-matched filler, and glue joints for extra holding power. When working with dark-stained crown, apply stain on the inside edges of miters so that any gaps won't show as prominently.

The easiest crown job. Because of the cathedral ceiling in this kitchen, the cabinet crown could be cut simply by registering its spring angles onto the miter saw's table and fence.

Work carefully with prefinished stock. To reduce visible nail holes, it's a good idea to use the smallest nail or brad possible when attaching crown or other exposed trim.

Backing not included. Finished trim panels on the back of peninsulas often require extra nailing support. Layout lines on the walls help to locate blocking in the right places.

Keep fasteners concealed. Meant to be covered by corner trim or base, the perimeters are good spots to attach the panels and still keep the appearance clean.

Build Your Own Bathroom Vanity

JUSTIN FINK

The details of a bathroom make a statement, and a vanity is often a focal point that ties those details together. The simplicity and clean lines of Shaker-style furniture appeal to me because they aren't adorned with excessive trim, appliqués, or other embellishments, yet they are more inviting and comfortable than modern pieces in a starker style. In addition, I think the Shaker style can work as well in a suburban raised ranch as it does in a 200-year-old farmhouse.

To build this vanity, you don't need a cabinet shop, and you don't need weeks of build time. With some common power tools and a slight increase in cost, you can build a vanity that is stronger and far more stylish than a production model, and that requires only a couple of weekends to complete.

A classic look with a lot less effort

When designing this Shaker-inspired piece, I started with the same height, depth, and compatibility with standard plumbing fixtures that would be present on a store-bought vanity. From there, I added some details that you won't easily find, such as mortised butt hinges, full-extension ball-bearing undermount drawer slides, a solid-wood top, and a traditional milk-paint finish. Compared to the details on a production-line vanity, these small changes can make a big

Make sheet goods more manageable. A track saw is ideal for dividing sheets of plywood into smaller, rough-size pieces. A sheet of 1-in.-thick rigid foam is a perfect sacrificial base and support for cutoffs. Run the parts through a tablesaw for final sizing to ensure that matching parts are the same dimension.

difference in the overall feel of the finished project, and they aren't that hard to execute. My goal in building this type of project is to respect the principles of traditional woodworking but challenge some of the techniques to make the building process a bit less fussy. Although the drawing on p. 144 may look intimidating, the necessary techniques for this build are basic, and I've included tips and tricks to increase your accuracy. The result is a vanity that looks and feels like a handcrafted piece of furniture, but one that goes together with more ease.

The most luxurious tools I used here were a track saw and a thickness planer, but even those are negotiable. If you don't have a track saw, then you can break down sheet goods with a circular saw and a homemade cutting guide. Also, even though you may be purchasing rough lumber that requires planing on its face and edges, most hardwood suppliers will do this work for a reasonable rate (my supplier charges 25¢ per bd. ft.) if you don't have a thickness planer.

Fastened, but left loose. After screwing together the two pieces of plywood for each center divider and attaching the spacers to each end panel, tack the subassemblies to the cabinet bottom with 16-ga. nails. Nailed sparingly, the case parts are loose enough for adjustment once the face frame is attached.

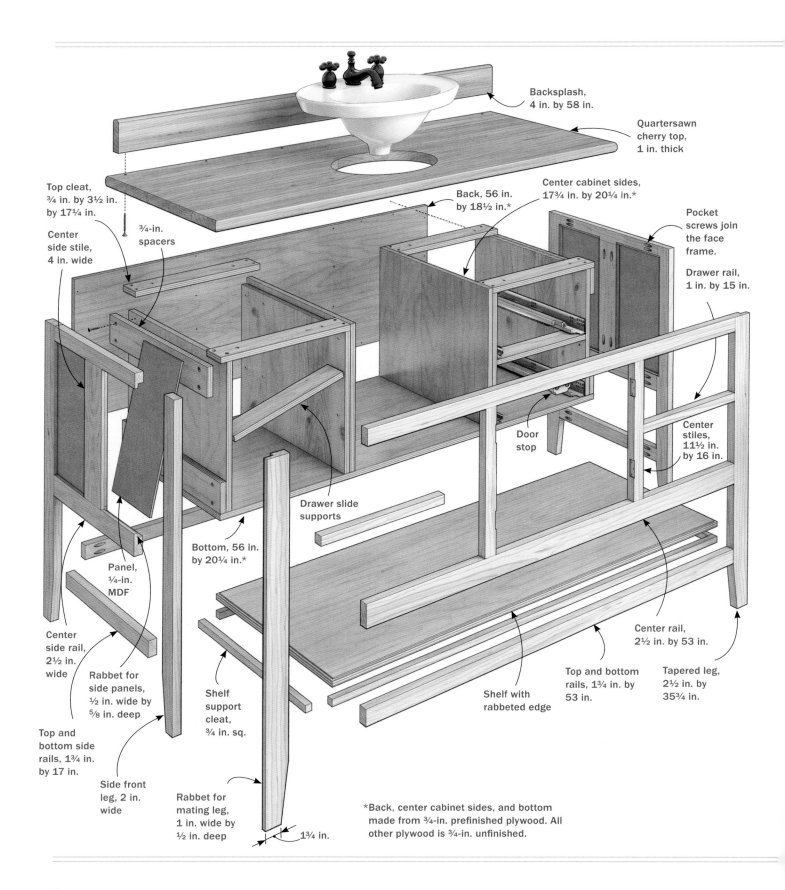

Backsplash,
4 in. by 58 in.

Quartersawn
cherry top,
1 in. thick

Top cleat,
¾ in. by 3½ in.
by 17¼ in.

¾-in.
spacers

Center side stile,
4 in. wide

Back, 56 in.
by 18½ in.*

Center cabinet sides,
17¾ in. by 20¼ in.*

Pocket
screws join
the face
frame.

Drawer rail,
1 in. by 15 in.

Center
stiles,
11½ in.
by 16 in.

Door
stop

Panel,
¼-in.
MDF

Drawer slide
supports

Bottom, 56 in.
by 20¼ in.*

Center
side rail,
2½ in.
wide

Rabbet for
side panels,
½ in. wide by
⅝ in. deep

Shelf
support
cleat,
¾ in. sq.

Shelf with
rabbeted edge

Top and bottom
rails, 1¾ in. by
53 in.

Center rail,
2½ in. by 53 in.

Tapered leg,
2½ in. by
35¾ in.

Top and
bottom side
rails, 1¾ in.
by 17 in.

Side front
leg, 2 in.
wide

Rabbet for
mating leg,
1 in. wide by
½ in. deep

1¾ in.

*Back, center cabinet sides, and bottom
made from ¾-in. prefinished plywood. All
other plywood is ¾-in. unfinished.

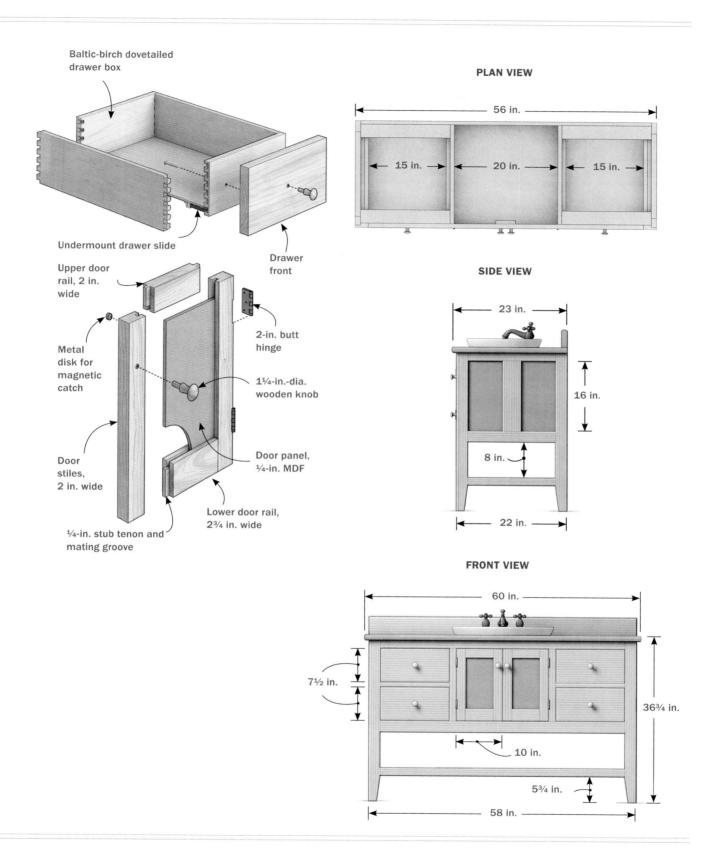

Baltic-birch dovetailed drawer box

Undermount drawer slide

Drawer front

Upper door rail, 2 in. wide

Metal disk for magnetic catch

2-in. butt hinge

1¼-in.-dia. wooden knob

Door stiles, 2 in. wide

Door panel, ¼-in. MDF

¼-in. stub tenon and mating groove

Lower door rail, 2¾ in. wide

PLAN VIEW

56 in.

15 in.   20 in.   15 in.

SIDE VIEW

23 in.

16 in.

8 in.

22 in.

FRONT VIEW

60 in.

7½ in.

36¾ in.

10 in.

5¾ in.

58 in.

One part sizes the others. A sacrificial miter-saw fence and shopmade throat plate ensure cleaner cuts. They also make it easy to register the stock, so you only have to measure the first piece in each group of parts, which can then be laid atop the next piece for repeat cuts.

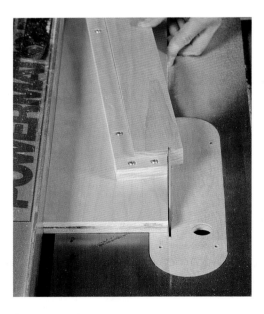

Quick and clean tapers. The bottom of each leg stile receives a taper cut to give the finished vanity the look of a stand-alone piece of furniture. A plywood jig with an L-shaped fence allows the piece to be safely supported for a clean-cutting pass on the tablesaw.

Materials chosen for their strengths

The build starts with the cabinet's plywood case, which is the foundation of the entire vanity—the part to which the rest of the components will be attached. The case consists of a continuous bottom piece, upright dividers to separate the center cabinet from the drawer sections that flank it, and a continuous back that locks everything into place. You'll need one sheet each of unfinished and prefinished ¾-in. plywood.

The unfinished plywood is used for the areas of the vanity that will either be painted or remain unseen. For water resistance and overall longevity of the undersink area, I prefer to use prefinished plywood. If you can't find a source for prefinished plywood, I recommend finishing both sides of a sheet of plywood with several coats of polyurethane and letting it cure before cutting the sheet into pieces. Otherwise, it can be a hassle to apply and sand clear coats of finish on the inside of an assembled box.

The joinery used in the plywood case won't be visible in the final piece; for that reason, you can use a finish nailer to tack most of the parts together. After assembling the face frame and attaching it to the boxes, lock the plywood together permanently with 2-in. screws.

Aside from the plywood used for the bottom shelf, all of the surfaces of the vanity that will be painted are built from 5/4 poplar (1-in. finished thickness) and ¼-in. MDF. Both of these materials are readily available, inexpensive, and stable, and they take paint well.

For the top of my vanity, I decided to use solid quartersawn cherry. Compared to more conventional flatsawn lumber, quartersawn boards have relatively straight-running grain, an inherently stable orientation that minimizes movement across the surface of the wood as its moisture content changes.

An ideal spacer. When assembling the front face frame, use the drawer fronts—which are cut to the exact size of the opening—to help align the stiles and rails. Later, trim the drawer fronts to their slightly smaller finished size and you will have wasted no extra material on throw-away spacers.

Faux floating panels. To achieve the look of true floating panels without all of the complex joinery, assemble each of the vanity side-panel frames with pocket screws, and then cut a ½-in.-wide by ⅝-in.-deep rabbet in the back side of the poplar stiles and rails to accept a ¼-in. MDF panel.

The order matters. Because they are only tacked together, the plywood parts have room for adjustment, which allows you to bring the case and assembled frame into alignment. First, flush up and fasten the two long rails, then the two outermost stiles. Follow up with the inner stiles and then the drawer rails.

Pocket holes are fast and strong

The parts for the face frame, side-panel frames, legs, doors, and drawer fronts are all cut at the same time. All are crosscut to 1 in. longer than their final desired lengths, ripped ⅛ in. wider than their desired width, and then run through the thickness planer on all four sides to bring them to their final dimension before crosscutting them to their exact length.

Anywhere that I can, I use pocket-screw joinery as a fast and strong solution for hidden fastening. A pocket-hole jig is quick to set up, a cinch to use, and with hardly any moving parts, it just never seems to let me down. The only places on this project where I used a more traditional form of joinery were on the two doors.

Because the doors incorporate floating panels, the surrounding poplar pieces need to be grooved on a tablesaw to accept the ¼-in. MDF panels. But pocket screws won't work when driven through a groove-edge board, and even if they did work, the exposed grooves and pocket holes would be visible when the cabinet doors were open.

Instead, cut stub tenons on the edges of the doors' top and bottom rails, allowing them to fit into the same groove that is already being cut to accept the MDF panel. All of this joinery can be cut on the tablesaw, provided you carefully set the fence and blade height for each step. After glue-up and sanding, trim the doors to fit.

One setup, two passes. Door stiles and rails receive ½-in.-deep grooves made by cutting to one side of a marked centerline, then flipping the piece to widen the ⅛-in. kerf into a ¼-in. groove. A featherboard ensures that parts stay firmly pressed against the fence.

Nibble the tenons. A stop block attached to the fence of a miter gauge registers each end of the door rails to create the shoulder cut of the ½-in.-long stub tenons, which are created by making a series of successive passes and testing the fit in the mating groove.

Not loose or tight, but snug. The panel and tenons should slide snugly into the grooves. If the tenons are too thin, glue shims to their cheeks. If they're too fat, hit them with a sanding block. After glue-up, trim the door to final height.

Mortises made easy. After trimming the top and bottom of the doors, rout the hinge mortises on the doors and assembled face frame using a T-shaped plywood template and bearing-guided mortise bit.

One door marks the other. With the first door sized, hung, and clamped in the closed position, temporarily hang the second door and mark a line on the back side where the doors overlap.

Double-stick sled. The safest way to trim the second door, especially if the cut needs to be a slight taper, is to attach the door to a plywood sled with double-faced tape so it can be cut on the tablesaw.

Tackle the gluing in stages. Rather than trying to glue up a 23-in.-wide countertop all at once, glue up pairs of boards. This makes it easier to get parts clamped and misalignments corrected before the glue starts to set up. Join the pairs to make the whole top.

Know when to buy rather than build

Drawer boxes aren't much harder to build than any other part of this vanity. But when I compare the convenience and low cost of ordering dovetailed drawer components with the steps and amount of time involved in making them myself, it's a simple decision. I buy my drawer components online from Barker Door, where the parts are cut to my specifications and arrive ready for glue up and finishing. For this project, the parts for all four drawers made of Baltic birch (a type of tightly veneered plywood) cost me $143, including shipping to my doorstep. Had I bought the plywood and built the boxes

myself, I would have spent $116 for materials alone, and I consider my time worth more than the $27 savings.

For drawer slides, don't skimp. It's the one part of this cabinet that gets used daily, so it's the last place you want to save a buck. I use Blum undermount slides. They aren't cheap, but they install easily, ride smoothly, and have a soft-close mechanism.

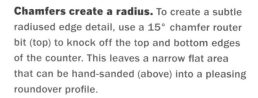

Chamfers create a radius. To create a subtle radiused edge detail, use a 15° chamfer router bit (top) to knock off the top and bottom edges of the counter. This leaves a narrow flat area that can be hand-sanded (above) into a pleasing roundover profile.

Perfect drawer faces. With the drawer boxes fixed to their slides and pushed into the cabinet, apply double-faced carpet tape to the back of the drawer face and carefully press it into place. The tape is strong enough to allow the drawer to be opened so that the front can be fastened from the inside of the box with 1¼-in. pan-head screws.

Step up to a solid-wood top

For the top of my vanity, I bought rough-dimensioned 6/4 cherry boards and planed them to a 1-in. finished thickness. After gluing up and sanding the top, I cut the hole for the sink using a template and a jigsaw before applying the polyurethane finish. This sequence is important because it allows me to apply finish to the visible surface of the countertop and also to the edges of the sink cutout, which are likely to get wet at some point in the life of the vanity.

This vanity took about 30 hours to complete and cost me about $850 in materials—comparable in cash outlay to many commercially available vanities of this size and style. In fact, this vanity was less expensive than many similar models being sold online. Plus, I know mine is built solid in a classic style that I believe will remain timeless, and it has a handmade touch that you can't get from a factory-built vanity.

Sources

Drawer boxes
Dovetailed Baltic birch, unassembled
www.barkerdoor.com

Knobs
1¼-in.-dia. Shaker knob
www.shakerworkshops.com

Drawer slides
563H undermount slides
www.barkerdoor.com

Hinges
2-in. rolled barrel butt hinges
www.horton-brasses.com

Faucet
Kingston Brass KS395.AX
www.faucetdirect.com

Sink
Kohler K-2075-8-0 Serif
www.amazon.com

Paint Milk Paint
Soldier Blue
www.milkpaint.com

Replace Your Vanity

TYLER GRACE

My business specializes in interior renovations, so I'm no stranger to gutting an old bathroom and building it from the studs and subfloor back to a fresh finished space. But in many cases, all that's needed is a facelift to bring the aesthetics into the current decade. Typically, such jobs involve new flooring, trim, plumbing fixtures, lighting, and the cherry on top of the updated finishes: a new vanity.

At its core, the workflow for replacing a vanity is pretty straightforward—turn off and disconnect the plumbing, yank the old vanity out, put the new vanity in, and reconnect the plumbing—but the devil is in the details. If you want the work to look and function at a professional level, there are some subtle steps to the process. You have to know the tricks for removing the old vanity without causing unintended damage, and how to fit the new one without relying heavily on shims and caulk. Moreover, some cautionary knowledge about the plumbing will go a long way toward ensuring that you won't need to make multiple trips to the store for plumbing parts, and that leaks won't ruin all your hard work.

1. Plan on spillage. There will be water in the faucet supply lines and a slug of dirty water sitting in the drain trap. Keep things dry by setting a bucket on top of a towel.

2. Plug the drain pipe. After removing the sink trap, use a rag or a reusable drain plug to block sewer gases from wafting into the room.

3. Slice the seams. To minimize drywall damage, cut the caulk around the cabinet and countertop with a sharp utility knife.

4. The top goes first. Use a stiff prybar to separate the countertop from the cabinet, and lift the whole top, complete with faucet, from the old vanity.

Methodical demo

Removing the old vanity is straightforward work, but these tips on sequencing and site protection will ensure that the task goes smoothly and doesn't risk damaging the rest of the room. First and foremost, before starting the demolition, unpack the new vanity and inspect it for defects or damage, and double-check measurements to be sure that the location of the existing plumbing will be compatible with the placement and size of the new cabinet. You don't want to discover that you chose the wrong replacement vanity after the old one is already sitting at the curb for trash pickup.

5. Prep the pipes. Escutcheons will interfere with the old cabinet removal and new cabinet installation, so remove them with metal-cutting snips.

6. Screws are last. Back out the screws holding the cabinet to the wall studs, being careful not to strip their heads.

7. Up then out. When removing the cabinet, lift up and away from the wall, being careful not to bend plumbing stub-outs.

How Much Filler Do I Need?

The vanity will come with a filler strip that is wider than necessary, allowing you to rip it to whatever width you need. That width is determined by the countertop overhang and by how far from flat and plumb your wall is. If the wall is relatively plumb, attach the filler strip and then rip it to leave an extra ⅛ in. for doing the final scribe later.

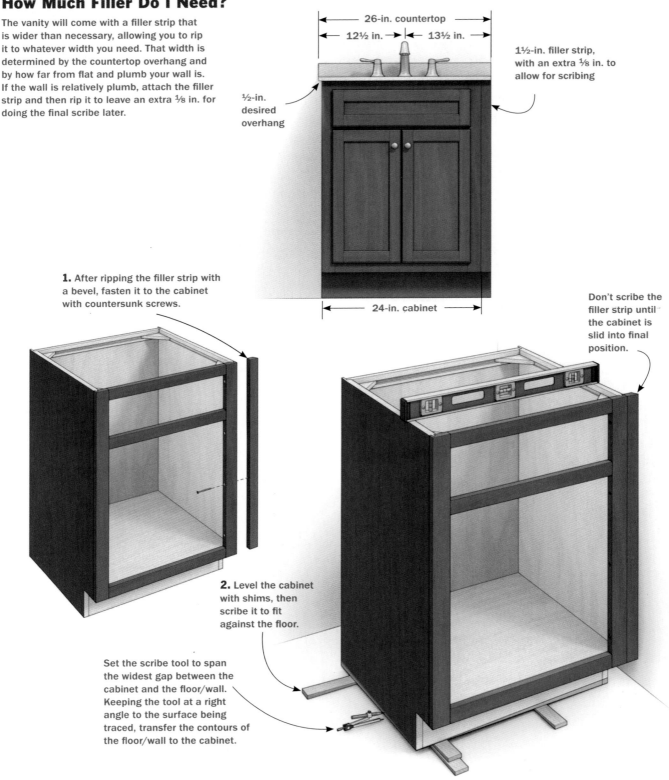

26-in. countertop

12½ in.

13½ in.

1½-in. filler strip, with an extra ⅛ in. to allow for scribing

½-in. desired overhang

24-in. cabinet

1. After ripping the filler strip with a bevel, fasten it to the cabinet with countersunk screws.

Don't scribe the filler strip until the cabinet is slid into final position.

2. Level the cabinet with shims, then scribe it to fit against the floor.

Set the scribe tool to span the widest gap between the cabinet and the floor/wall. Keeping the tool at a right angle to the surface being traced, transfer the contours of the floor/wall to the cabinet.

Fit the cabinet

Scribing—a transferring technique used to cut the cabinet for a perfect fit against the walls and floor—elevates the quality of your vanity installation and eliminates the need to caulk and to hide irregularities created by shimming. For vanity cabinets that have a solid back, this process needs to be done in two phases: an initial scribe to level the cabinet and fit it against the side wall, and then, after the back has been cut so that it can be slid into position against the back wall, a second round of scribing for a final fit. The process isn't hard to learn, but the sequencing has to be correct.

3. Use a level to span the gap. Slide the cabinet as close to final position as the plumbing stub-outs will allow, then set a level across the cabinet to mark where its top edge will contact the rear wall.

4. Establish a reference line. Pull the cabinet out of the way and then extend the level line across the wall from that point.

5. Measure and record. Measure each pipe position relative to two points—the corner of the wall and the horizontal reference line—then mark the measurements on the wall.

6. Transfer to the cabinet back. Using the cabinet's side and top edges as your reference points, mark the location where each pipe will protrude through the cabinet back.

7. Holes in two steps. Drill penetrations using a hole saw slightly larger than the diameter of the pipes. Start from the back side, stopping when the pilot bit pokes through, then use that hole to position the drill bit to finish the hole from the inside.

8. Scribe the back edge. The drilled holes allow the cabinet to slide into final position against the back wall, where it can be shimmed level and then scribed along the back edge of the side panel so it fits tight to the wall.

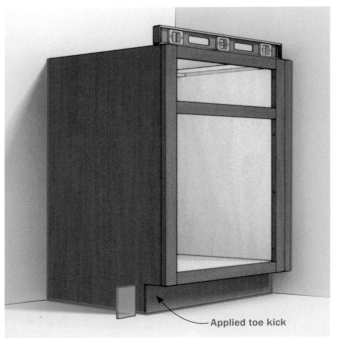

Applied toe kick

9. Final scribing. With the cabinet in place, do a fine-scribe along the side where it meets the floor and wall, and scribe the bottom and right end of the applied toe kick before cutting the excess from the left end and installing.

10. Shim the gap. Fasten the cabinet to the rear wall with screws long enough to penetrate at least 1½ in. into the studs, being sure to drive them through the fastening rail near the top edge. When fastening to the side wall, add scraps of wood and/or shims to match the width of the scribed filler strip.

Countertop and plumbing come last

Install as much of the faucet plumbing as you can prior to setting the countertop. This not only reduces the gymnastics of working in a dark, cramped vanity cabinet, but it also makes it easy to ensure that the handles and spout are aligned correctly and spaced evenly. When installing the drain assembly, don't reuse parts from the old vanity. The cost savings would be minimal, but even if drain parts were expensive, it still would not be worth the potential for leaks. On that note, you can leave the cabinet empty for a few days just to make sure there are no leaks. It's easier to adjust a drain trap or snug up a compression fitting than to replace an entire vanity because of an unnoticed leak.

Get a good mark. A strip of painter's tape makes a pencil-friendly path for marking hard, glossy countertops with a scribe tool.

Sand to fit. Solid-surface counters can be cut and shaped with carbide tools and then sanded down to a scribe line using an angle grinder equipped with a sanding disk.

Easy access. It's much easier to install and align the faucet before setting the countertop than it is to reach underneath after it's installed.

Wet set. After confirming that the countertop scribe fits the wall, apply adhesive caulk to the inside edge of the cabinet to avoid visible squeeze-out as the top is set and taped into place to cure.

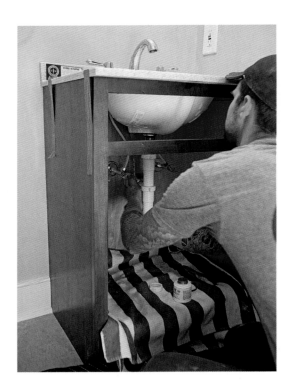

Prepare before plumbing. It pays to spend the time planning what you need up front; otherwise, you'll spend it making multiple drives to the home center or plumbing store for the parts you forgot.

Undersink Success

Most faucet packages include all of the components you see from the finished side of the sink, and sometimes even supply lines. The rest of the drain assembly and optional escutcheons must be purchased separately.

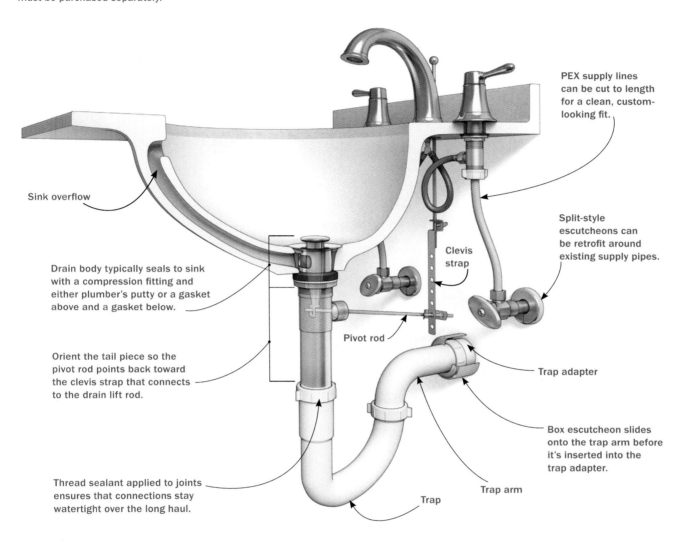

PEX supply lines can be cut to length for a clean, custom-looking fit.

Sink overflow

Split-style escutcheons can be retrofit around existing supply pipes.

Drain body typically seals to sink with a compression fitting and either plumber's putty or a gasket above and a gasket below.

Clevis strap

Pivot rod

Orient the tail piece so the pivot rod points back toward the clevis strap that connects to the drain lift rod.

Trap adapter

Box escutcheon slides onto the trap arm before it's inserted into the trap adapter.

Thread sealant applied to joints ensures that connections stay watertight over the long haul.

Trap arm

Trap

Beautiful Cases from Plywood

CRAIG THIBODEAU

A lot of articles have been written about making veneered panels with a vacuum bag. Most of these take you as far as trimming the panel and popping it into a door frame, or maybe applying edging and turning that panel into a tabletop. Those techniques are important, but there's much more you can do.

I've been building entire case pieces with veneered panels for years. With them, I can make pieces that are simply not possible with traditional methods. I love the creative freedom: the variety of exotic woods and dramatic figure available, the ability to make patterns with these veneers, and then being able to wrap these woods and patterns around an entire piece. Another great benefit of veneered panels is that I can give the interior of a case a completely different look.

Although there is not a lot of information available on building furniture this way, I've learned how to make the process easy and the results flawless. The first secret lies inside the panel itself.

The core is the heart of the method

How you build with veneered panels depends a lot on what they're made of. The usual candidates for core materials involve a trade-off. Baltic-birch plywood, for instance, is very strong and stable and holds fasteners well, but it's expensive and heavy. MDF, which I used for years, is cheap and offers an exceptionally smooth surface for veneering, but it weighs even more than Baltic birch and isn't as good structurally.

When I got tired of wrestling heavy sheets, I experimented until I came up with the best of all worlds: a manageable panel that can vary in thickness but is always rigid, stable, and flat. The heart of this custom substrate is ¾-in.-thick lumber-core plywood. It is relatively light but strong. The solid-wood core makes everything easier. The long grain along the edges creates excellent glue joints, and the whole panel takes fasteners well, such as splines, screws, biscuits, and more.

To this core I typically add a skin of ⅛-in.-thick MDF on each side. This gives me the perfect surfaces I need for veneering. If I want thicker panels I use ¼-in. MDF for the skins or add a second layer of lumber core in the center.

Making custom cores doesn't take much extra effort: it's just one more glue-up before the veneering stage. I cut the parts 1 in. oversize in each direction, so alignment isn't critical. I apply yellow glue to one face of each layer, and then put the sandwich in the vacuum bag for an hour or two. Then I apply the veneer in a separate step. One helpful tip is to leave one edge of the lumber-core plywood slightly proud so it can be used as a reference edge when trimming the panel to final size later.

For thinner case components like doors and drawer dividers, I go back to simple Baltic-birch plywood as the substrate. It's available

(Continued on p. 166)

Two Approaches, a World of Possibilities

Thibodeau builds veneered furniture in two ways, framed by solid wood
or mitered seamlessly. Either way, the veneer is a design playground,
allowing techniques not possible in solid wood.

FRAMED BY SOLID WOOD

MITERED CASES

Better Substrate for Veneering

Thibodeau's main substrate is lumber-core plywood skinned with thin MDF. Lumber-core is relatively light but holds glue and fasteners better than other sheet goods. MDF thickens the panel and creates a flawless surface for veneering. For thinner parts like doors and dividers, he veneers directly onto Baltic-birch plywood.

CUSTOM CASE PANELS

¾-in. lumber-core plywood   ⅛-in. or ¼-in. MDF   Veneer

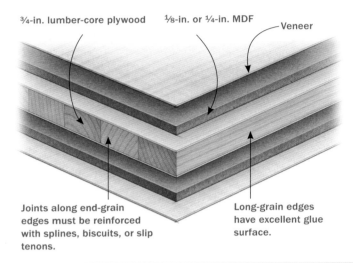

Joints along end-grain edges must be reinforced with splines, biscuits, or slip tenons.

Long-grain edges have excellent glue surface.

SOLUTION FOR THINNER PARTS

Baltic-birch plywood, any thickness

Veneer grain runs perpendicular to plywood face grain.

Before applying veneers, one extra step. Leave everything oversize at this point, but leave one edge of the plywood core slightly proud to act as a reference edge when trimming the panel later. Apply glue to just one face of each layer using a ¼-in.-nap adhesives roller.

Vacuum bag is fast and easy. Thibodeau uses evacuation cloth to transfer the vacuum from the hose inlet to the glue-up and evacuation mesh to distribute the air pressure evenly. Both are available from www.vacuum-press.com (product Nos. EVC38 and EVN36).

Frame-and-Panel Case:
New Method for a Traditional Look

Thibodeau uses customized veneered panels and clever joinery to build a frame-and-panel case. He varies the thickness of the parts to create reveals and shadow lines on the outside. Inside, he keeps everything flush for a seamless interior.

THREE DIFFERENT THICKNESSES
A ⅛-in. reveal between each part creates attractive shadow lines.

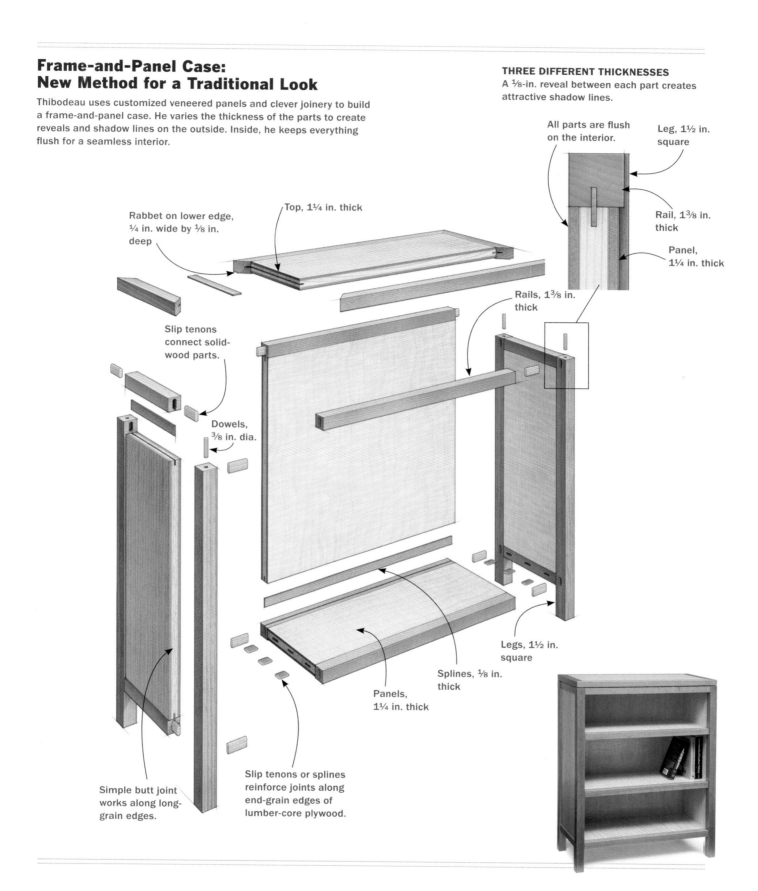

All parts are flush on the interior.

Leg, 1½ in. square

Rail, 1⅜ in. thick

Panel, 1¼ in. thick

Rabbet on lower edge, ¼ in. wide by ⅛ in. deep

Top, 1¼ in. thick

Slip tenons connect solid-wood parts.

Rails, 1⅜ in. thick

Dowels, ⅜ in. dia.

Legs, 1½ in. square

Splines, ⅛ in. thick

Panels, 1¼ in. thick

Simple butt joint works along long-grain edges.

Slip tenons or splines reinforce joints along end-grain edges of lumber-core plywood.

in a variety of thicknesses. For a stable panel, be sure to run the veneer grain at right angles to the grain on the face of the plywood. These thin components tend to have exposed edges, which I veneer first before veneering the faces.

Frame the panels for a traditional feel

The bookcase on p. 165 illustrates how I use solid-wood members to frame veneered panels. When using this frame-and-panel anatomy, I vary the thicknesses of the parts to create reveals (little steps), while keeping everything flush on the inside surfaces to make joinery easier and the interior seamless. It's the best of both worlds: a traditional look on the outside and a nice surprise within. Make things easier on yourself by sanding all of the parts before assembly. By the way, the outside panels on this piece are curly anigre, the interior is curly maple, and the shelves are also curly maple, edged with cherry.

I always build the side assemblies first, because they act as a foundation for the rest of the piece. The solid rails at the top and bottom of each panel are secured using full-length splines, a few small Domino tenons, or biscuits. I join the side assemblies to the legs using slip tenons inserted into the rails (the mortises can extend into the panel, too). You don't need splines along the sides of the panel, though you could use them to ensure alignment. The lumber-core plywood has long grain on those edges, so a simple glued butt joint is plenty strong.

It doesn't matter how you cut the mortises that join the rails to the legs, but it's important to reference off the interior surfaces so the parts end up flush there. These days I use the Domino system throughout my veneered pieces, but before that I used a simple router template (see p. 168 for a photo).

With a router jig, there is more measuring and marking to get the locations and reveals right. The Domino requires far less fussing and you can work with the panels and assemblies flat on the benchtop. The Domino centers its mortises on ¾-in.-thick stock (or close to it), but all it takes is a thin piece of MDF or plywood to shim it up for thicker panels and pieces.

At this point the top of the case is open. The actual top, with its edges framed with mitered solid-wood pieces, is simply doweled down onto the case. To be sure all the dowels line up, I use an elegantly simple guide, one of my favorite jigs (see the drawing on p. 170).

The top seems to float, but that effect is created simply by cutting a small rabbet into its lower edge.

Mitered corners for a seamless look

The liquor cabinet on p. 171 is another example of the fun you can have with veneer. The main veneers and solid-wood parts are walnut, while the top panel, the interior, and the panels I cut into the sides and doors are curly anigre. The little detail beads are wenge. These window inlays wouldn't be possible in solid wood. I cut them after the cabinet was assembled, to be sure they lined up, and used a router template for the job.

Start with the side panels. These frame-and-panel assemblies are the foundation for the rest of the piece. When cutting the joinery, Thibodeau references off the inside face, where everything should end up flush. Attach the rails first. A simple butt joint won't work on the end-grain edges of the plywood. Groove the rails and panels on the router table using a slot-cutting bit.

Glue in splines. For full strength, cut the splines so the grain runs across the short dimension.

Trim everything to width. Now rip both edges clean on the panel-and-rail assemblies. The plywood panel was left proud on both sides to ride the rip fence effectively. Thibodeau puts blue tape on the leading and trailing edges to prevent blowout.

Add the legs. Slip tenons run between all the solid-wood parts in this cabinet. When cutting the tenon mortises, always reference off the inside surfaces. The Domino is as easy as a biscuit joiner, and the parts can usually lie flat on the bench. The Domino is designed to center joints on ¾-in. plywood, so shim it up for thicker parts.

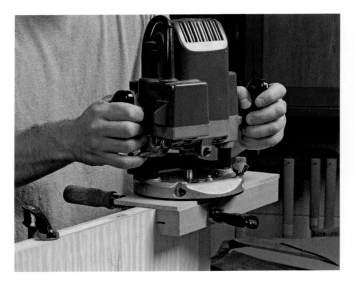

Router option. Another way to tackle the mortising is to use a plunge router equipped with a guide bushing and spiral upcut bit. A slotted template clamped to the workpiece guides the router.

Glue on the legs. Thibodeau protects the pre-sanded legs with cauls. Check that the tops of the legs and back of the panel end up flush. A dead-blow mallet corrects any misalignment.

Add the bottom and back. Glue on the rails, and then trim each panel to final width. Cut the mortises for the slip tenons that will join them to the side assemblies. Here Thibodeau uses the Domino system, but splines or biscuits would work, too. Make an L by joining the back and bottom, which share a rail. Check for squareness with an accurate framing square, making adjustments by shifting the clamps slightly. Again, use cauls to protect sanded surfaces.

This cabinet showcases my other favorite method of joinery for veneered work. Its main box—the back, two sides, and the narrow solid edging that surrounds the doors—is built with miter joints.

The case then goes onto a base that is made up of a bottom panel surrounded by a frame, with legs doweled from below. The top's anatomy is just like the one on the bookcase, except that it is beveled on its lower edge instead of sitting on a rabbet. Both top and bottom are attached with dowels, using the same type of drilling guide I made for the bookcase.

It all starts with the mitered case. I use a sliding tablesaw to cut the long miters, but careful setup of a conventional tablesaw can produce clean bevel cuts. Attach a sacrificial fence to your rip fence and bury the blade in the fence at 45°—exactly at the height of the thickness of the panel. Take time to get the fence perfectly aligned so the blade cuts a clean miter without taking anything off the top face. Otherwise, the workpiece will dive inward as you finish the cut, creating a gap in

Transfer the joinery. Dry-fit the back and bottom assembly onto one of the sides, and transfer the joinery locations from one assembly to the other (left). Thibodeau uses an MDF or plywood panel as a fence for the Domino. He uses a saddle square to transfer the tick marks to the fence (above).

Add one side at a time. Attach one side, clamp it, and let it dry. Then add the front rail and the final side as shown. Again, cauls protect the sanded surfaces.

Fence ensures perfect alignment. Thibodeau uses the Domino vertically against the fence, following the tick marks.

Doweling Jig Lines up the Top

A few dowels are all you need to align and attach the case top. Since it is a veneered panel, wood movement is not an issue. A slick drilling jig lines up the dowel holes.

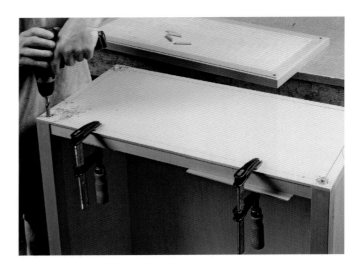

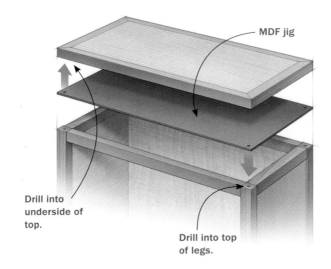

MDF jig

Drill into underside of top.

Drill into top of legs.

Case first. Cut a piece of MDF the same size as the case, and mark it so the holes will land squarely in the legs. Clamp the jig to the case and drill. Put tape on the bit to set the depth. Clamp the jig to the top to drill shallower holes into its underside.

the joint. To dial it in perfectly, use a cutoff section of one of the actual panels, and then cut one more piece to make sure two miters add up to a clean, square joint. Also, make sure all of the parts are trimmed to final size before beveling them.

Safety note: The offcut will be trapped between the blade and fence, and it does shoot out sometimes, so stand out of the way as you make the cut.

I made the two narrow stiles that flank the doors from solid walnut, veneering the door fronts with vertically oriented walnut veneer to create continuous grain across the front of the cabinet.

Front is actually four parts—The front of this cabinet is different from the previous one, with stiles that take the place of the solid posts and a veneered top rail that attaches to those stiles before final assembly. There is also a solid center stile, which goes in as the top and bottom are added to the case. So after mitering the edges of the side stiles, use more slip tenons to attach the upper rail that connects

them. That rail is solid walnut, veneered on both sides, with the grain running vertically for invisible seams with the side stiles.

My favorite part about the miter approach is assembly. You simply apply packing tape tight along the outside of the pieces, add glue, and then fold up the miters to clamp them. I usually don't reinforce the miters with splines, since they have so much long-grain glue surface already. This is just another place where the lumber-core plywood is a big benefit.

Easy corner inlay—I sometimes inlay a strip of solid wood, like the wenge I used here, into the corners of mitered cabinets. These small details add flair, protect the veneer from dings and damage, and hide a not-so-perfect miter. You can notch the corners of small boxes on the tablesaw, but for big casework like this I use a handheld router and a rabbeting bit.

Once the case is done, build the base and top to fit, and then attach them using dowels and a drilling guide.

Mitered Case: Miters are Strong and Seamless

To wrap veneer seamlessly around an exterior, Thibodeau uses mitered joinery. This system is very fast, and the lumber-core plywood creates strong joints without the need for splines.

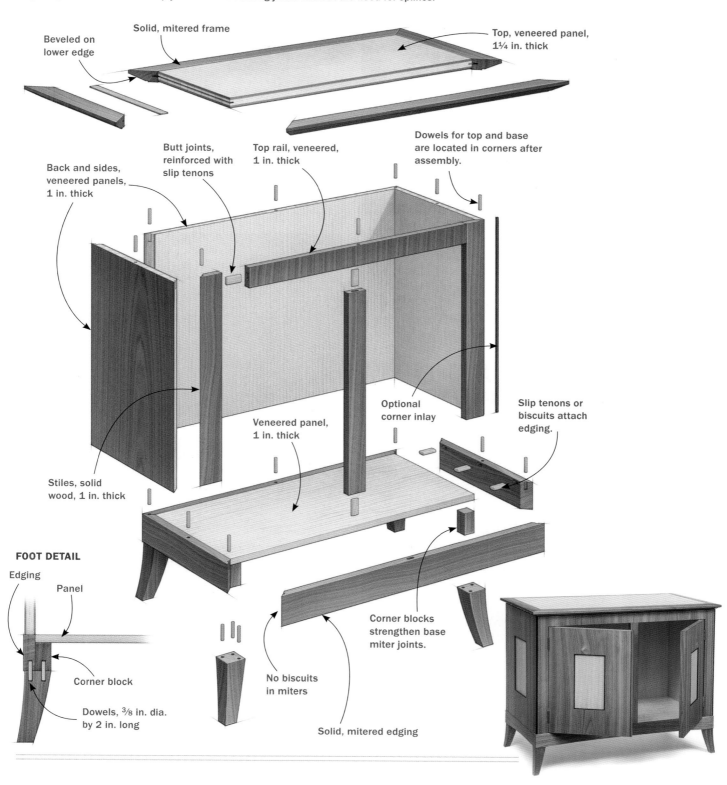

Beveled on lower edge

Solid, mitered frame

Top, veneered panel, 1¼ in. thick

Butt joints, reinforced with slip tenons

Top rail, veneered, 1 in. thick

Dowels for top and base are located in corners after assembly.

Back and sides, veneered panels, 1 in. thick

Optional corner inlay

Slip tenons or biscuits attach edging.

Veneered panel, 1 in. thick

Stiles, solid wood, 1 in. thick

FOOT DETAIL

Edging

Panel

Corner block

Dowels, ³⁄₈ in. dia. by 2 in. long

No biscuits in miters

Corner blocks strengthen base miter joints.

Solid, mitered edging

Flip 'em and tape 'em. Flip all the parts outside-face up, stretch clear packing tape across each joint, and then run long pieces down each one to add strength and stop squeeze-out.

Simple approach to a fussy joint. Thibodeau cuts case miters at the tablesaw, burying the blade in a sacrificial fence. It takes some trial and error to fine-tune the setup, but the results are flawless. If the workpiece wanders, or you don't press it down near the blade, you won't ruin the edge. Just make another pass to ensure a clean miter.

Stick trick. It's hard to turn over all of the parts without loosening the tape, but two sticks make it easy to grip and flip the panels.

Glue and fold. Brush a thin layer of glue on all of the mitered surfaces, and then fold up the whole assembly and add the front rail (center above). Throw a clamp across that rail, and then add a spacer and clamp at the bottom of the cabinet to be sure the whole thing comes together square (above).

Corner Inlay Is a Nice Touch

If your miter joints have a few gaps or you want a contrasting detail, it's easy to add solid inlay to the corners.

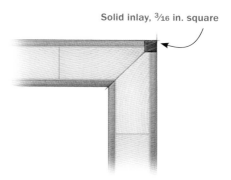

Solid inlay, 3/16 in. square

Rout a rabbet. Use the smallest router you have and either an edge guide (shown) or rabbeting bit to cut a square recess in the edge. Start with a shallow climb cut to avoid tearout.

Tape trick. Cut the edging just a hair oversize. Strips of blue tape are all the clamps you need. Stretch them to pull the inlay tight in its channel. Trim the inlay flush after the glue dries.

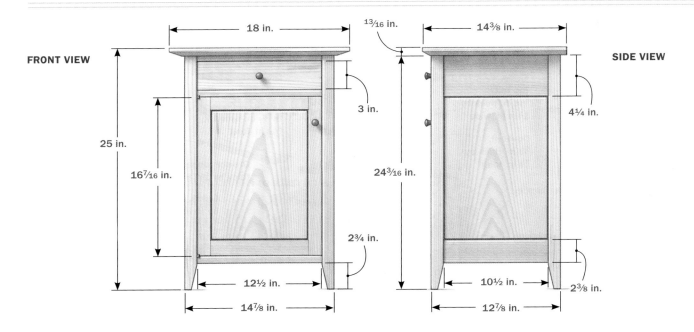

FRONT VIEW

18 in.

25 in.

$16\frac{7}{16}$ in.

$12\frac{1}{2}$ in.

$14\frac{7}{8}$ in.

3 in.

$2\frac{3}{4}$ in.

$\frac{13}{16}$ in.

SIDE VIEW

$14\frac{3}{8}$ in.

$4\frac{1}{4}$ in.

$24\frac{3}{16}$ in.

$10\frac{1}{2}$ in.

$12\frac{7}{8}$ in.

$2\frac{3}{8}$ in.

CUT BOTH CHEEKS

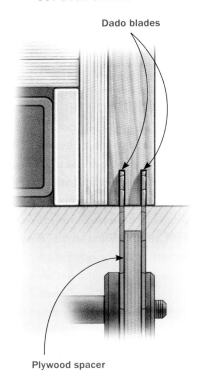

Dado blades

Plywood spacer

To mark the side and back rail grooves, insert a rail into a leg and transfer the groove location to the rail with a knife. Then re-adjust the cutter height, add a fresh zero-clearance fence, and groove the rails.

With the leg joinery done, taper the feet at the bandsaw and clean up the sawmarks with a handplane. Now it's time to focus on the connections at the front of the case.

Handling the rails

The front rails connect to the legs in two ways. The top rail is dovetailed into each leg and the lower two rails are double-tenoned into the legs.

I cut the dovetails in the top rail on the bandsaw. I also cut a shallow rabbet under the tail so I have a shoulder to register against the leg. To get the shoulder-to-shoulder length of all three front rails, mark them directly off a rear rail. This will keep the case square. To cut the sockets, transfer the tail to the leg, then saw down the lines as far as you can. Drill most of the waste and pare with a chisel to fit the joints. Cut the mortises for the lower rails, then cut and fit the tenons.

Tenons at the tablesaw. Rousseau cuts the cheeks at the tablesaw using the two outer blades from a dado set with a plywood spacer between them (see the bottom drawing on the facing page). He uses dado shims to dial in the cut for perfectly sized tenons.

Mitered where they meet. The tenons on the upper and lower rails are mitered where they intersect in the rear legs. Rousseau cuts the miters at the tablesaw.

Size the panels and fit the bottom

With the bones of the case fitted, the next step is the panels. When cutting the panels to final dimension, be careful to note the season and adjust the fit for expansion and contraction. Cut a rabbet around each panel at the router table with a rabbeting bit and a zero-clearance fence. I use a short 1¼-in.-dia. router bit made by Whiteside (No. 1304). With the sides and back panels fitted, move on to the case bottom.

The bottom is held by grooves in the lower case rails and a rabbet in the lower front rail. I cut the rabbet so that the bottom will sit slightly proud, creating a solid stop for the door. Make the rear rail's groove deeper to allow room for seasonal movement.

To mark for the rabbet in the lower front rail, assemble one side rail and the lower front rail into a leg, and transfer the groove from the side rail to the front rail. After cut-

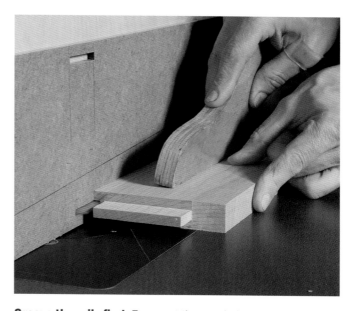

Groove the rails first. To accept the panel, the rails are grooved with a wing cutter at the router table. A piece of thin brownboard, used as a zero-clearance fence, keeps the bit from tearing out the piece.

Now groove the legs. To cut the grooves in the legs, start by marking the fence with the position of the cutter. Place the cutter into the mortise for the rail tenons—which is wider than the wing cutter—to start the cut. End the cut inside the opposite mortise and turn off the router before removing the workpiece.

Take care of the feet. Cut the tapered feet at the bandsaw. A simple jig ensures consistent cuts.

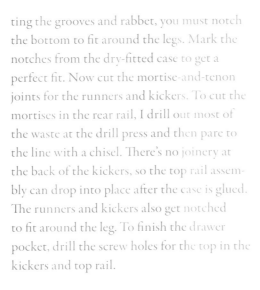

ting the grooves and rabbet, you must notch the bottom to fit around the legs. Mark the notches from the dry-fitted case to get a perfect fit. Now cut the mortise-and-tenon joints for the runners and kickers. To cut the mortises in the rear rail, I drill out most of the waste at the drill press and then pare to the line with a chisel. There's no joinery at the back of the kickers, so the top rail assembly can drop into place after the case is glued. The runners and kickers also get notched to fit around the leg. To finish the drawer pocket, drill the screw holes for the top in the kickers and top rail.

Top rail gets dovetailed. Although the lower front rails are attached to the legs with double tenons, the top rail is dovetailed in. The dovetail is shouldered on the underside, which makes it easy to register the piece against the leg for marking.

Mortise for the knife hinges

Installing knife hinges can be tricky. But I use a cool method for marking the mortises that makes it easier to see where to cut.

Start by placing a piece of blue tape where the hinge will go, then use double-faced tape to attach the hinge in its exact location. Knife around the hinge and remove the hinge along with the blue tape beneath it. You'll be left with a perfect outline of the mortise.

Using a laminate trimmer with a ⅛-in. straight bit, rout out the bulk of the mortise. Get as close as possible to the blue tape and finish squaring the edges with a chisel. When you've cut the hinge mortises in both rails, it's time to get out the glue.

Plan the glue-up carefully

Before going through a dry run of the glue-up, apply finish to the panel tongues and the frame edges. Finishing these parts now will eliminate the hassle of getting finish into the crevices later. When the finish is dry, walk through the glue-up without the glue. Once you feel confident, glue up the sides first. Check each side frame for square and be sure the panel is centered in the frame.

Mortise for the Knife Hinges Before Assembly

Knife hinges are a simple yet elegant way to hang a door. Making sure the mortises for these hinges are cut accurately can be daunting, but here's an easy way to get crisp, tight-fitting mortises with just a bit of tape.

Cut through the blue tape. After placing double-faced tape on the back of the hinge and pressing it firmly in place on the rail, knife around the hinge. When the hinge is pulled off, it will lift the cut piece of blue tape, leaving a perfect outline of the mortise.

Rout out, then pare. Remove the majority of the waste with a trim router and ⅛-in. spiral bit. Clean up the shoulders with a chisel.

A small dab of glue in the center of the top and bottom rail groove will keep the panel in position after glue-up.

With the two sides dry, glue the remainder of the case together. This includes the rear rails, the rear panel, the bottom panel, the lower two front rails, and the runners. Again, a dry run is very helpful.

In this wave of the glue-up, don't glue in the top dovetailed rail, just set it in dry. Make sure the clamps are parallel to the rails; otherwise, it's very likely they'll rack the case out of square. At this point, make sure all of the joints are tight.

With everything together, check for squareness along the case front, back, and top. I use a tape measure on the outside dimension, or a folding ruler with a slide on the inside. Once the case is square, clean up any squeeze-out.

Finish the web frame

The next step is to take care of the drawer pocket. Before the dovetailed rail and the kickers get glued in, glue in the guides, which ensure that the drawer slides in straight. They're simply two pieces of wood planed down to fill the gap between the leg and the side rails. Dial in their fit so they're flush to the front leg, and glue them in with a couple of spring sticks (see the top photo on p. 182). Now, glue in the kickers. To make sure they're parallel with the runners, make two Masonite® spacers for them to register against. The dovetailed top rail and kickers are glued and clamped into place.

Fit the door, drawer, and top

The frame-and-panel door is built like the other panels. It's important to make the door slightly larger than the opening so it can be trimmed to fit. Again, pre-finish the panel and then glue it up.

Once it's dry, use a handplane to fit the door to the opening. In my experience, most cases are not perfectly square. But the eye is drawn mostly to the reveal around the door, so if the door is planed to create an equal gap, no one will ever know. The size of the washers on the knife hinges equal the reveal size.

While the hinge mortises in the rails butt right up to the legs, the door-side hinges must hang over the edge of the door to create a reveal. To set the overhang, use a shim made of layers of blue tape to offset the hinge mortise location.

Cut the mortises in the door and fit the hinges. The brass screws supplied with the hinges break easily. To avoid this, I always pre-drill the holes and then cut the threads with a steel screw. For added security, I wax the brass screws before final installation. Once the door is installed, you can make any adjustments to that last reveal between the door and leg.

The drawer has half-blind dovetails on the front with through-dovetails at the rear—fairly standard construction. I build all my drawers slightly oversize in width and then handplane them for a piston fit.

The top of the case is beveled on the underside of the front and sides to lighten its appearance. I cut the bevels on the tablesaw using a tall fence with the blade at an angle. The top is screwed to the case via pre-drilled and slotted holes in the kickers.

Choosing the right finish

The European beech I used for this cabinet really called for a finish that wouldn't alter the wood's tone. For this piece, I wiped on Osmo Polyx™ hardwax oil. After that, I waxed and rubbed out the finish with a piece of burlap.

Sides first. In a multi-panel case, it's important to tackle the glue-up in stages. Start by gluing up the individual sides, making sure they're square and the panel is centered in the frame. To make things easier later, finish the panel edges (above left) and frame grooves before gluing things together.

Fill in between the sides. Once the sides are dry, join them with the case bottom, lower front rails, and the rear panel and rails. The dovetailed rail at the top is only dry-fitted at this stage (above left). While it's still in the clamps, check the case for square (above right). If the case needs to be adjusted, the clamps can be tilted slightly to apply pressure to rack it back into square.

Stick clamps.

Keep the socket parallel.

Seat the rail and kickers.
After the tenons on the ends of
the kickers are glued into the
mortises on the dovetailed top
rail, put the whole assembly
in place on top of the waxed
spacers.

Lock it in place. A handful of
clamps is enough to get a good
bond between the kickers and
the side rails. Be sure to clamp
along the dovetailed top rail
as well.

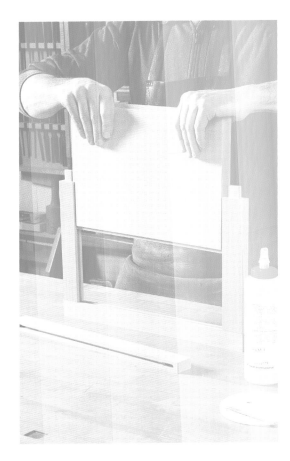

Get the door together. The door is built just like the sides of the case—mortise-and-tenons for the frame and a groove along the inside for the panel.

Size for the reveal. The door should be built larger than the opening, and then cut to leave consistent reveals top to bottom, side to side.

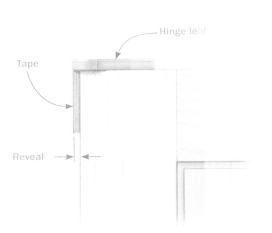

Hinge leaf

Tape

Reveal

Space out the door's hinge mortises. Apply a reveal to the hinge side of the door to prevent binding. Use a folded piece of blue tape. Each leaf for the hinge should overlap the paper thickness.

Hinges in order. Install the hinge halves in the case first (above left), then on the top of the door (above right). Make sure the threads in the case and door are drilled and pre-cut with a steel screw before driving in the brass screws.

1. Put upper hinge pin into the case.

2. Slide lower hinge half into mortise in bottom of door.

Slide it into place. To get the door in place, start by putting the upper hinge pin into the case. Then slide the lower hinge half into the mortise in the bottom of the door. Now, adjust the final fit of the door and set the ball catch (9 mm ball catch, No. 241.86.105, www.hafele.com) before screwing the hinge in place.

SHELVES AND BOOK-CASES

3-D Shelves Enliven Any Room

DAN CHAFFIN

I first made these simple wall-hung display boxes for my home. Since then, I have made a lot of them for clients, who like the boxes because they can be grouped in geometric patterns to create beautiful, modern, and highly functional storage. Each box hangs on a French cleat, hidden behind the back of the box. The cleat is super-strong, so you can load up the box with books, pottery, and whatever else you want without worrying about it crashing down.

The boxes are simple enough to make (see the drawing on p. 188). The challenge is hanging a group of them in an accurately spaced pattern, because once you put the box on the wall, you no longer have access to the cleat to make adjustments.

Fortunately, I have a creative business and shop partner, Matt Frederick. He had the idea to use a "mounting box" to hang the wall cleat. This mounting box is a 3-D template sized to match the outside dimensions of the actual box, but it's half as deep and has no back—just a cleat that mates to the wall cleat. This backless design allows me to hang the wall cleat with a single screw, set the mounting box on it, locate and level the box precisely, and then drive in the remaining screws that hold the wall cleat in place.

The mounting box is very easy to make (see the drawing on p. 191). It's just butt joints and screws. The cleat is attached with screws driven in through the box sides. I'll show you how to use it to arrange the display boxes in any pattern.

Stack and hang. A clever mounting method makes it a cinch to stack and arrange these simple boxes.

Installation is easy

After making the mounting box and the wall cleat, you can hang the box. First, figure out where you want it on the wall and mark for the top edge of the wall cleat. To hang an array of boxes, you'll need to plan more to figure out the spacing between the boxes. After you have determined that space, hang a box in the lowest row first, and then work your way up the rows.

Align the top edge of the wall cleat with a pencil mark on the wall and attach it with a

Wall of Storage

Individually, these boxes are simple and understated, but arranged geometrically on the wall they become as striking as they are useful.

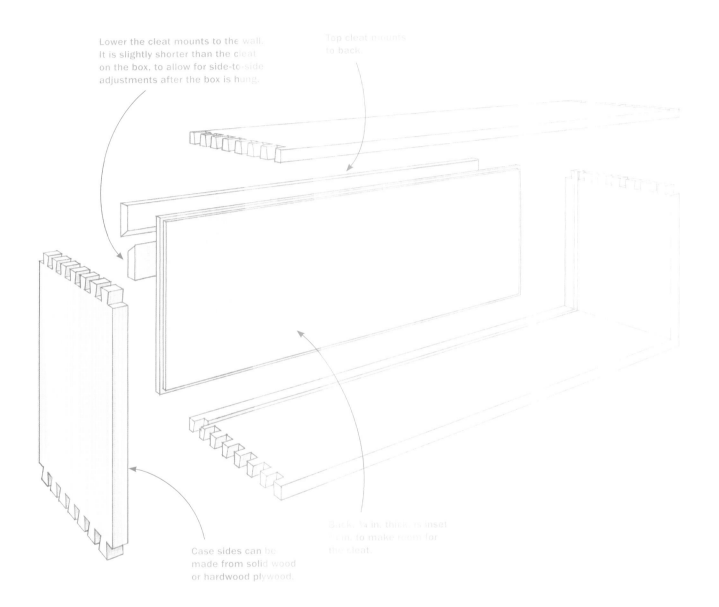

Lower the cleat mounts to the wall. It is slightly shorter than the cleat on the box, to allow for side-to-side adjustments after the box is hung.

Top cleat mounts to back.

Case sides can be made from solid wood or hardwood plywood.

Back, ¼ in. thick, is inset ¼ in. to make room for the cleat.

Hang man. To help arrange and hang the boxes on the wall, Chaffin uses a backless box. The box makes it easier to lay out the 3-D shelves and install the French cleats that they mount to.

Beveled Cleats Anchor the Shelves

The French cleat is a great way to hang the boxes because it's strong and easy to make. All you need are two strips of ¾-in. hardwood or plywood with a mating beveled edge.

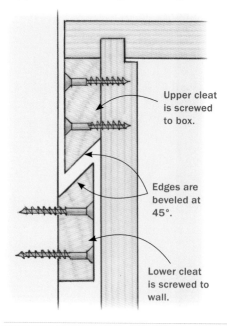

Upper cleat is screwed to box.

Edges are beveled at 45°.

Lower cleat is screwed to wall.

single screw in the center. Set the mounting box on the wall cleat and place a level on top of it. Adjust the box until it is level, then drive in the remaining screws to anchor the cleat to the wall. Remove the mounting box and put the display box in place. You're done.

There are two ways to locate the remaining boxes after you've hung the first. For big distances, such as the spaces between boxes on the horizontal rows of this pattern, measure from a hung box to the mounting box. Hold the second box's wall cleat against the wall, set the mounting box on it, and then have a friend measure between them. For small distances, like the spaces between the rows, I use a spacer. I place it on top of a box in the lower row and set the mounting box on top of it. The cleat on the mounting box will show you where to put the wall cleat.

Attach the cleat to the back.
For better support, make it long
enough to just fit between the
box sides, and the screws it hold
against the box to screw. Next,
the cleat to the box with two
of screws (left).

Mounting Box Is the Secret

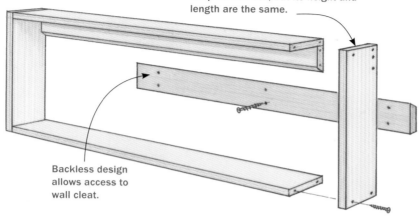

Mounting box, made from ¾-in. plywood and assembled with screws, is half as deep as wall box, but its height and length are the same.

Backless design allows access to wall cleat.

1

Hassle-free hanging. Attach the wall cleat first, using just one screw in the center (1). Hang the mounting box on the wall cleat (2). Level the box and drive the rest of the screws into the cleat (3). If possible, drive into studs; otherwise, use wall anchors. When hanging multiple rows of boxes, it's easiest to start at the bottom.

2

3

The mounting box stands in for the real thing.

Make a Country Hutch

ANDREW HUNTER

When I'm making furniture for others, I build in all sorts of styles. But when a piece of furniture is for my own house, I go country. Having grown up in New England, I am partial to the simple pine furniture of our northern settlers. This cupboard, with its open top and decorative cutouts on the sides, has its design roots in the 17th century.

Like the original makers, I worked my white pine boards unplugged. Don't get me wrong—I don't build everything by hand. But I really enjoy using hand tools, and when I'm making a piece for myself, I like to indulge a little and skip the machines. The pleasure of the handwork shows in the finished piece, and it feels good knowing all that has gone into making it.

When building a piece with hand tools, it is best to keep things simple. This cabinet relies primarily on nails for its strength. The box-joined top, along with the dadoed shelves, bottom, and counter, are fixed with nails through the sides, and nailed face frames and cross struts reinforce the structure. With the back boards nailed in place at every horizontal, this cupboard is rock-solid. I use traditional cut nails, and I don't hide them. The exposed nail heads are appropriate to the country style, and the contrast between the silky-smooth pine and hard steel looks great.

Handsome Cupboard

Nailed dadoes, notches, and
box joints make the cabinet
straightforward to build but very
strong.

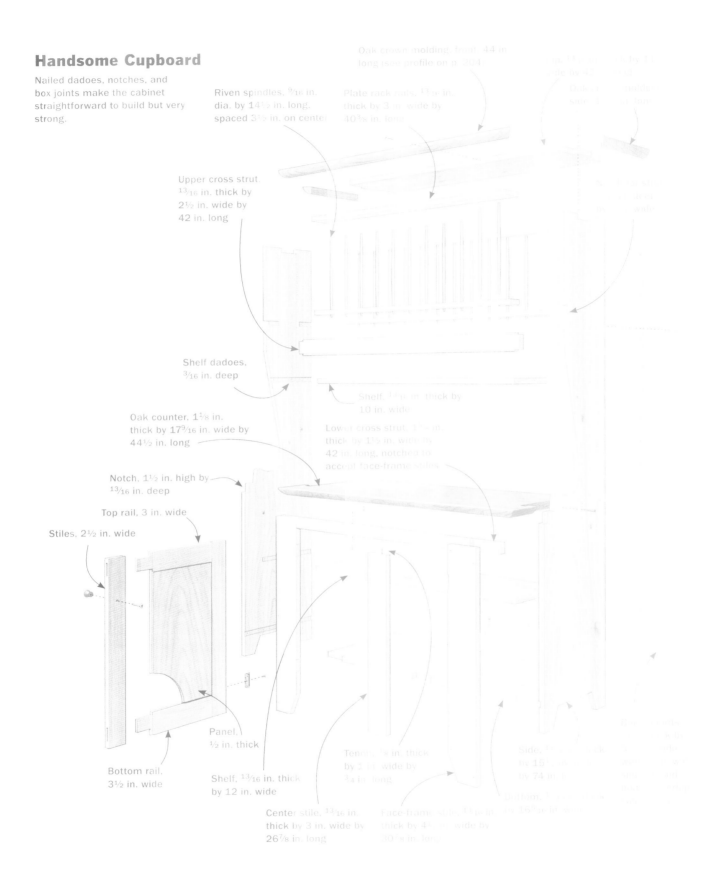

Oak cross molding, front, 44 in.
long (see profile on p. 204)

Riven spindles, 9/16 in.
dia. by 14 1/2 in. long,
spaced 3 1/2 in. on center

Plate rack rails, 13/16 in.
thick by 3 in. wide by
40 3/8 in. long

Upper cross strut,
13/16 in. thick by
2 1/2 in. wide by
42 in. long

Shelf dadoes,
3/16 in. deep

Shelf, 13/16 in. thick by
10 in. wide

Oak counter, 1 1/8 in.
thick by 17 9/16 in. wide by
44 1/2 in. long

Lower cross strut, 13/16 in.
thick by 1 1/2 in. wide by
42 in. long, notched to
accept face-frame stiles

Notch, 1 1/2 in. high by
13/16 in. deep

Top rail, 3 in. wide

Stiles, 2 1/2 in. wide

Panel,
1/2 in. thick

Bottom rail,
3 1/2 in. wide

Shelf, 13/16 in. thick
by 12 in. wide

Center stile, 13/16 in.
thick by 3 in. wide by
26 7/8 in. long

Face-frame stiles, 13/16 in.
thick by 4 in. wide by
30 3/8 in. long

Tenon, 1/4 in. thick
by 2 in. wide by
3/4 in. long

FRONT VIEW

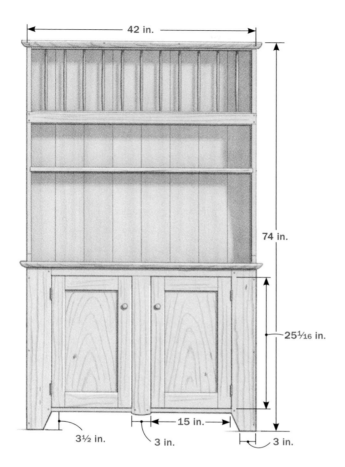

42 in.

74 in.

25 1/16 in.

15 in.

3 1/2 in.

3 in.

3 in.

SIDE VIEW

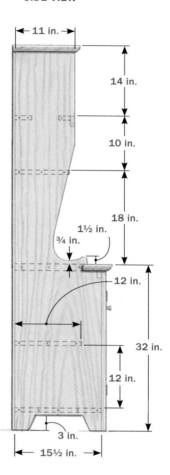

11 in.

14 in.

10 in.

18 in.

1 1/2 in.

3/4 in.

12 in.

32 in.

12 in.

3 in.

15 1/2 in.

DOOR PULL

1 in. dia.

1 1/8 in.

11/16 in. dia.

I used red oak for the counter, upper molding, spindles, and door pulls. I like red oak and white pine paired together. I left the pine without finish, but used tung oil to bring out the oak's rich color.

I painted the back boards with slate-blue milk paint. This allowed me to use inferior boards for the back while creating a uniform background for the dishes on display.

Start with the sides

I began the hutch by ripping and crosscutting all the parts a bit oversize, then milling them flat. I cut parts to final size only as needed during the build. You can mill your boards by machine, of course, but I flatten rough boards by hand.

The curved cutouts in the sides give this hutch its individuality, and you can design a profile to suit your own tastes. I sawed out the bulk of the waste with straight ripcuts and crosscuts. Then I cut the curve with a bowsaw and cleaned up to the lines with a handplane and spokeshave. I used that completed side as a template to draw the cutout on the second side.

To make the foot cutouts, start with angled ripcuts, use a bowsaw to make the horizontal cut, and clean up with a chisel.

Cut the dadoes—All the major horizontal surfaces except the top are set into dadoes in the sides. I used a Japanese panel saw to make the parallel kerfs that establish the width of the dadoes. The saw's small curved head makes following a guide block simple and lets you start or end a cut in the middle of a board, as with the stopped dadoes. Once you've made the sawcuts, excavate the waste with a chisel. Clean up the bottom of the dado with a long chisel or grooving plane.

Box joints at the top—To secure the top to the sides, I chose a three-part box joint secured with nails. It provides multi-directional strength not offered by a nailed rabbet, yet is far easier to lay out and cut than dovetails. The single tenon of the top is easily made with rip- and crosscuts, but the center notch in the side boards needs to be chopped with a chisel.

Notches hold the cross struts—The beaded cross strut at the bottom of the plate rack gets let into notches in the sides. Start those notches with multiple stopped sawcuts to the baseline, then chisel the rest of the waste. The lower cross strut, which is just below the counter and doubles as the top rail of the face frame, is also let into the sides, but those notches can be simply sawn out with a ripcut followed by a crosscut.

Cut the curves in the sides. Hunter makes the curved cuts in the sides with a bowsaw. After sawing, he smooths the curves with a plane and spokeshave.

One side mirrors the other. Use the first completed cutout as a template to draw the shape on the other side piece.

Dadoes for the shelves. Using a 90° guide block and a panel saw with a depth line drawn on the blade, make the kerfs that define the width of the dado.

Chisel out the middle. Remove most of the waste with the bevel down. Finish with a long chisel bevel up or a grooving plane.

Depth check. To be sure your dadoes reach proper depth, make a test piece that easily fits the dado and draw a line on it at full depth.

Box joint at the top. Saw out a pair of notches at the end of the top board to create a central tenon.

Matching notch. With saw and chisel, cut a central notch at the top of each side. Do the chopping and paring from both faces toward the middle to avoid blowout on the bottom face.

Make the shelves and counter

With the two sides finished, start the shelves and counter. To ensure consistency, lay out the shelves with a story pole and then cut and plane their ends to length. Test-fit the shelves in the dadoes and shave their bottom edges if the fit is too tight. For the counter, make the cutouts at the ends so the counter slides into its dadoes. But wait to cut the small notches that lock over the case sides until you've created the counter's edge profile.

Cut the profile with a smoothing plane. Shape the front edge first, taking straight, continuous shavings from end to end. As you near the profile line, take lighter passes. The final curve will be made up of many facets, which can be left visible or scraped smooth. I leave mine unscraped. Repeat the process on the two ends, working from the outside in to prevent blowout. Now cut the small notches.

CROSS-STRUT PROFILE

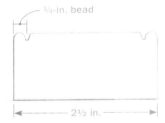

¼-in. bead

2½ in.

COUNTER PROFILE

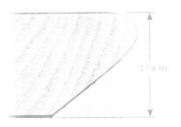

1⅛ in.

A place for plates

The plate rack consists of two separate frames, each with riven oak spindles captured between an upper and lower rail. I drilled holes for the spindles with a ⅜-in. tapered bit. The slight taper of hole and tenon makes it easier to get a snug fit. I split the spindles from a piece of straight-grained firewood and did most of the shaping with a drawknife while the wood was still green. Green wood works like a dream, and it only takes a few days to dry the spindles near the woodstove. I wanted a roughly faceted look, so I left the texture right off the drawknife. For a smoother surface you could do some final shaping with a spokeshave or block plane after the spindles dry.

With the spindles dry, taper their ends and fit them one by one to their holes. After fitting one end of a spindle, insert it in the rail and make a mark 12⅜ in. up the shaft. Then fit the other end so it seats to the mark. Once all the spindles are fitted, you can trim the ends flush. I let the bottom ends protrude because I liked the way they looked.

I used an antique molding plane to cut the beads on the upper cross strut, but a scratch stock would also work. After you cut the beads, trim them back at each end to fit the strut into its notches. Leave the strut long to prevent splitting when you nail it in. You'll saw the ends flush after assembly.

Cut the face frame for the cabinet

The face frame—the vertical and horizontal members that surround and divide the doors—helps ground the piece visually and adds rigidity to its structure. The top rail of the face frame—the lower cross strut—is twice as thick as the upper strut, because the stiles of the face frame must be notched into it. This strut also has a mortise to mate with the tenon of the vertical divider between

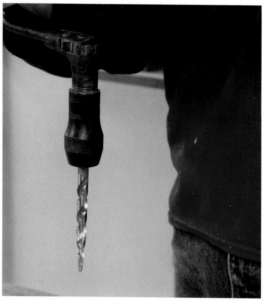

Plate rack. Using a tapered bit (right) to cut the holes for the spindles makes fitting them easier.

Split and shave. Firewood and a splitting ax produce the raw material for the spindles. A drawknife shapes the green wood quickly. Hunter leaves his spindles roughly faceted. You could refine yours with a spokeshave or handplane.

Taper the tenons. Fit the spindle ends one at a time to their holes, planing them to a taper. With one end of the spindles fitted, mark shoulder lines on the opposite end 12⅜ in. from the face of the rail. Taper the second end until it fits up to that line.

Set and secure the rack. Slide the front plate rack into place and then nail in the cross strut. Hunter drives nails up through the top rail of the rack into the top board of the cabinet.

Leave it long. To avoid splitting, leave the cross strut over-length until the nails are driven in. Then cut it flush to the case side.

Top trick. When nailing in the mitered molding at the top of the cabinet, Hunter temporarily tacks a scrap or two to the top board to help with alignment.

CROWN MOLDING

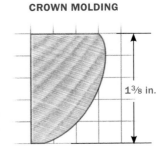

1⅜ in.

A New Approach to Classic Cabinets

MIKE MAINES

The room in the southwest corner of our 1830s Greek revival is by far the fanciest in the house, with its tall baseboards and door casing with flat planes meeting at an angle instead of the more common rounded field. Even the windows are fancy—at least by the standards of rural Maine—with the casings running to the floor and a flat panel under each that is finished to match the walls. The existing fireplace surround, however, was not very attractive.

My wife and I appreciate the history of our house, but we have no desire to live in a museum. So we decided it was time to design and build a fireplace surround, complete with a pair of bookcase cabinets, that would be honest to the spirit of the house but updated with a slightly modern feel.

Over the years, I've refined my approach to building cabinets without the luxury of a fully stocked cabinetry shop, so I knew this was a project I could tackle on site.

Modernizing the style

The design process involved a lot of sketches and scribbles, but it breaks down simply: The fireplace surround is proportioned to be stocky and proud, just like the house. The flanking bookcases have clean lines and flush surfaces. Meant to evoke classical columns, they look traditional without being fussy. The two pilasters (the legs of the mantel) sit on plinth blocks. The frieze (or lintel) projects beyond the pilasters by ¼ in., just like

Assembly should leave room for adjustment. If you've cut all the parts correctly, the face frame and the plywood should line up perfectly. Here's how to assemble the carcases when they don't. Start with nails. Tack the plywood box together with 15-ga. or 16-ga. finish nails. It will be a little floppy, but that's a good thing at this point.

Hidden attachment. After nailing the box together, align the long sides of the face frame to the cabinet, and fasten them with pocket-hole screws. The screws will be covered by end panels after installation.

Tap it into alignment. Use a hammer and block to tap the tops, bottoms, and any fixed shelves into alignment, then fasten them with pocket screws.

Secure it with screws. After everything is aligned, fasten through the sides of the cabinet with $1\frac{5}{8}$-in. screws. Shorter screws won't hold well, and longer screws may lead to splits.

Solid backs mean extra steps. After slotting the edge of each back board to receive a $\frac{1}{4}$-in.-thick plywood spline, fasten the boards with screws in a combination of countersunk and slotted holes to allow for seasonal movement.

Scribe for a tight fit. I usually leave a stile that will butt against a wall or other finished surface ¼ in. to ¾ in. wider than necessary so that it can be scribed for a perfect fit. After marking the scribe in place, I lay the cabinet flat on its back so that I can cut to the line and then finish the edge with a block plane.

Trim the fat. Use a track saw to remove as much wood as possible without reaching the scribe line. Back-cutting at a 30° bevel makes the hand-planing easier.

Finish with care. For a simple scribe, use a block plane to shave up to the line. Complicated scribes may need a jigsaw or an angle grinder with a sanding disk.

Traditional work can still use modern joinery

Although I considered using my Festool® Domino joiner to build the face frames, I ultimately opted for the speed and simplicity of pocket-screw joinery on these parts. I like to add a dab of glue to the joints; end-grain gluing only has one-tenth the strength of edge-grain gluing, but I think it contributes to the joint staying tight and not telegraphing through the paint.

For joining the plywood carcases, I used my no-fuss, adjustable method in which each box is constructed loosely and then tweaked as needed to fit the more-rigid face frame. I have tried every possible way to join face frames to carcases; my go-to method for paint-grade work is to glue the face frames on, tacking them in place with 18-ga. brad nails. The downside to that method is that the filled nail holes sometimes telegraph through the paint. Because our new house has an intermittently wet basement, I expect significant fluctuations in humidity, so I chose my "high-end" system of attaching the face frames with pocket screws.

The backs presented an unusual challenge. I typically use plywood because it's self-squaring and easy to attach with screws or narrow-crown staples. But solid wood needs room for seasonal movement. I bought the red birch planks roughsawn, then milled them to ¾ in. thick, straightened them with a track saw, and grooved their edges with a router. The groove was sized to accept plywood splines that hold everything in plane but still allow the solid boards to expand and contract. I drilled pilot holes in the perimeter and the center of each board, but to allow for expansion, I used the Domino to create elongated slots at each edge of the wider boards. All the boards are attached to the carcase with bugle-headed cabinet screws.

Doors that break all the rules. For this project, I tried a new technique for the doors. I used the Festool Domino tool to cut slots on all edges of the ¾-in. plywood panels, rails, and stiles, and on the ends of the rails. After cutting a rabbet around the panel to create a reveal, I glued the panels right in their frames. To start, arrange the door parts with their finished sides facing up. Draw a triangle in the center of the panel, then mark each stile and rail with the corresponding portion of the triangle that matches its position relative to the panel. Mark the same number in each triangle so that you know the grouping and orientation of each part.

Slots, not biscuits. In terms of layout and use, operating the Domino is very similar to operating a biscuit joiner. Mark both pieces where they will join, dial in the height and depth, and plunge the tool into each piece to create a matching slot.

A rabbeted shadowline. To disguise the joint between panel and door frame, and to create a nice reveal, rabbet the edges of each panel on the finished side. Hit the rabbets with spackle, primer, and a light sanding before assembly.

Glue and clamp. After inserting glue and tenons into the edges of the plywood panel, dab glue into the tenon holes of the stiles, rails, and along their edges. Position the rails first, repeat the process for the stiles, and then clamp everything together. Using a straightedge as a guide, adjust the position of the clamps to ensure that the doors are flat.

To attach the cabinets to the wall, I used #10 wood screws with finishing washers, placed to lower their visibility once the shelves were installed and loaded with books. I shimmed the cabinets adequately at the floor, so the screws in the wall aren't bearing any weight.

The cabinets and the trim are both finished with Sherwin-Williams®' All Purpose Latex Primer and topcoated with two coats of Benjamin Moore's Advance waterborne alkyd paint in a semigloss finish. I had planned to use my Graco® airless spray gun for the primer coat only, because I think a brushed finish is more appropriate for an old house like ours, but once I went through the effort to mask everything off, I decided to spray the two topcoats as well. The finish came out great, and I highly recommend the paint, which flows out better and dries harder than regular latex paints. My wife and I love the way the new fireplace surround ties the room together.

Plan for adjustability. Place the hinges with the horizontal holes on the door and the vertical holes on the cabinet, and you'll have some room for adjusting.

The tricks to quick butt hinges. I chose the BH2A series of butt hinges from Cliffside Industries because I like the adjustment offered by their slotted holes. When working with these butt hinges, I like to follow two tricks I learned from a local cabinetmaker. First, mortise the door only; the other leaf of the hinge will create a nice reveal. Second, don't bother with stopped mortises; cut them right from the front of the door through to the back. Plywood scraps are all that's needed to make a custom hinge jig. A router with a flush-bearing bit rides the jig to cut the through mortise.

Hang and adjust in place. With the hinges in place on the cabinet doors, hold the doors in position while you transfer the hinge locations to the face frame. Attach the door, and tweak as needed for a perfect close.

Credits

All photos are courtesy of *Fine Homebuilding* magazine (FHB), © The Taunton Press, Inc., or *Fine Woodworking* (FWW) magazine, © The Taunton Press, Inc., except as noted below:

Front cover: photo by Dillon Ryan (FWW). Back cover: left photo by Dillon Ryan (FWW), right photo by Michael Pekovich (FWW)

The articles in this book appeared in the following issues of *Fine Homebuilding* and *Fine Woodworking*:

pp. 5–10: Plywood for Woodworkers by Tony O'Malley, FWW issue 225. Photos by FWW staff. Drawings by Vince Babak (FWW).

pp. 11–15: The Language of the Lumberyard by Steve Scott, FWW issue 221. Photos by FWW staff. Drawings by John Tetreault (FWW).

pp. 16–24: Staying Safe on the Tablesaw by Marc Adams, FWW issue 233. Photos by Asa Christiana (FWW). Drawings by Christopher Mills (FWW).

pp. 25–30: Tips for Square Glue-Ups by Steve Latta, FWW issue 226. Photos by Mark Schofield (FWW). Drawings by John Tetreault (FWW).

pp. 32–40: A Built-In Corner Seating Nook by Joseph Lanza, issue FHB 225. Photos by Charles Bickford (FHB). Drawings by John Hartman (FHB).

pp. 41–43: Comfortable Dining Nooks by Joseph Lanza, FHB issue 225. Drawings by Joseph Lanza.

pp. 44–52: Built-in Breakfast Nook by Andrew Young, FHB issue 262. Photos by Justin Fink (FHB), except bottom photo p. 52 by Nina Johnson. Drawings by Christopher Mills (FWW).

pp. 53–61: Design the Perfect Pantry by Paul DeGroot, FHB issue 233. Photos by Brian Pontolilo (FHB), except photo p. 60 by Samuel Pontolilo. Drawings by Paul DeGroot.

pp. 62-71: Build a Kitchen Island by Rick Gedney, FHB issue 232. Photos by Patrick McCombe (FHB), except photo p. 62 by Charles Bickford (FHB).

pp. 72–74: Considerations for Kitchen Islands by Rick Gedney, FHB issue 232. Photo by Charles Bickford (FHB). Drawings by Martha Garstang Hill (FHB).

pp. 75–79: A Clever Island with Drawers by Joseph Lanza, FHB issue 239. Photos by Charles Bickford (FHB). Drawings by John Hartman (FHB).

pp. 80–91: Build Storage into Any Bed by Tony O'Malley, FWW issue 240. Photos by Ben Blackmar (FWW), except photos p. 80 and pp. 90-91 by Michael Pekovich (FWW). Drawings by Christopher Mills (FWW).

pp. 93–97: A Cabinetmaker's Kitchen by Charles Miller, FHB issue 223. Photos by Charles Miller (FHB). Drawings by Martha Garstang Hill (FHB).

pp. 98–105: Simple Hanging Cabinet by Christian Becksvoort, FWW issue 252. Photos by Anissa Kapsales (FWW). Drawing by Christopher Mills (FWW).

pp. 106–119: Bowfront Wall Cabinet by Matt Kenney, FWW issue 238. Photos by Steve Scott (FWW), except photo p. 106 by Michael Pekovich (FWW). Drawings by John Hartman (FWW).

pp. 120–131: Get to Know Semicustom Cabinets by Nena Donovan Levine, FHB issue 242. Photos p. 121, 122, 128 (bottom) courtesy Canyon Creek. Photos p. 123 (left), 128 (top three) courtesy Merillat. Photos p. 123 (right), 124-126 courtesy MasterBrand. Photo p. 130 courtesy Aristokraft®. Photo p. 131 courtesy Omega® Cabinetry.

pp. 132–141: Installing Semicustom Cabinets by Isaak Mester, FHB issue 241. Photos by Charles Bickford (FHB). except for photo p. 134 (top) by John Ross (FHB).

pp. 142–152: Build Your Own Bathroom Vanity by Justin Fink, FHB issue 252. Photos by Rob Yagid (FHB). Drawings by John Hartman (FHB).

pp. 153–161: Replace Your Vanity by Tyler Grace, FHB issue 262. Photos by Aaron Fagan (FHB). Drawings by Christopher Mills (FHB).

pp. 162–173: Beautiful Cases from Plywood by Craig Thibodeau, FWW issue 247. Photos by Asa Christiana (FWW). Drawings by Christopher Mills (FWW).

pp. 174–185: Frame-and-Panel Cabinet by Timothy Rousseau, FWW issue 256. Photos by Dillon Ryan (FWW), except for product photo p. 179 by John Tetreault (FWW). Drawings by John Hartman (FWW).

pp. 187–192: 3-D Shelves Enliven Any Room by Dan Chaffin, FWW issue 240. Photos by Matt Kenney (FWW). Drawings by Vince Babak.

pp. 193–204: Make a Country Hutch by Andrew Hunter, FWW issue 242. Photos by Jonathan Binzen (FWW). Drawings by John Hartman (FWW).

pp. 205–213: A New Approach to Classic Cabinets by Mike Maines, FHB issue 244. Photos by Brian McAward, except photo p. 205 by Nat Rea.

Contributors

Marc Adams runs one of the largest woodworking schools in North America. Go to www.MarcAdams.com for more information.

Christian Becksvoort is a *Fine Woodworking* contributing editor and an expert in Shaker design.

Dan Chaffin is a professional furniture maker in Louisville, Ky.

Paul DeGroot (www.degrootarchitect.com) is an architect in Austin, Texas.

Justin Fink is the editor of *Fine Homebuilding*.

Rick Gedney is the owner of Kitchens by Gedney in Madison, Conn.

Tyler Grace is a *Fine Homebuilding* ambassador and the owner of TRG Home Concepts in Haddon Heights, N.J.

Andrew Hunter designs and builds custom furniture in Accord, N.Y.

Matt Kenney is a senior *Fine Woodworking* editor.

Joseph Lanza (www.josephlanza.com) designs and builds entire houses, as well as their parts, in Duxbury, Mass.

Steve Latta is a *Fine Woodworking* contributing editor who teaches furniture making at Thaddeus Stevens College in Lancaster, Pa.

Nena Donovan Levine is a kitchen designer in West Hartford, Conn.

Mike Maines is a designer, builder, and woodworker in Palermo, Maine.

Isaak Mester has been in the construction business for 28 years. Although he has tackled all phases of residential construction, he has concentrated on kitchens and baths during the last 10 years. In an acknowledgment of his sore shoulders and knees, Isaak has become a licensed building, electrical, and plumbing inspector.

Charles Miller is a *Fine Homebuilding* editor at large.

Tony O'Malley makes custom built-ins and furniture in Emmaus, Pa.

Timothy Rousseau is a furniture maker in Appleton, Maine, and a regular instructor at the nearby Center for Furniture Craftsmanship.

Steve Scott is a former *Fine Woodworking* associate editor.

Craig Thibodeau is an award-winning furniture maker in San Diego.

Andrew Young is co-owner of Young & Son Woodworks in Portland, Ore.

Index

A
Adams, Marc, 16–24, 216

B
Bathroom vanity, building, 142–52
  about: overview of, 142–43
  assembling/gluing, 147, 149, 150–52
  drawer boxes/faces, 150–51
  drawings, 144–45
  faux floating panels, 147
  joinery, 146, 148–49
  materials for strength, 146
  pocket-screw joinery and pocket holes, 148
  quick, clean tapers, 146, 149
  sizing parts, 146
  solid-wood top, 152
  sources, 152
Bathroom vanity, replacing, 153–61
  about: overview of, 153
  counter and plumbing install, 159–61
  demo process, 154, 155
  filler strip width, 156
  fitting, setting cabinet, 157–58
  holes for plumbing, 157–58
Becksvoort, Christian, 98–105, 216
Bed, storage in, 80–91
  about: overview of, 80
  adding base, assembling bed, 88–91
  assembling case, 83–86
  biscuit joints, 83–85, 86
  drawers and slides, 86–88
  drawings, 82, 86, 87
  edge-banding hiding plywood, 81
  false-front trick, 91
  gluing up clamp-free, 85
  modular design advantages, 82, 90
Board feet, explanation of, 12
Bowed lumber, 15
Box shelves. *See* Shelves, 3-D box
Breakfast nook. *See* Nook, built-in breakfast
Built-ins. *See also Nook* references

C
Cabinet, bowfront wall, 106–19
  about: overview of, 106–07
  bending/gluing plywood for doors/drawers, 112–17
  bent-lams for drawer fronts, 116, 117–19
  curve types (three), 108–09
  doors and drawers, 112–19
  drawings, 108–09, 113, 114
  routing curves, 110–12
Cabinet, frame-and-panel, 174–85
  about: overview of, 174
  assembling, 181–85
  building case frames, 174–76
  cutting mortises and tenons, 174, 177
  drawings, 175
  finishing, 180
  finishing web frame, 180
  fitting door, drawer, top, 180
  mortising knife hinges, 179
  planning glue-up, 179–80
  rails, 176–77
  sizing panels and fitting bottom, 177–78
Cabinet, simple hanging, 98–105
  about: overview of, 98
  design options, 99
  double roundover, 101
  dovetail joinery with pins, 100, 103
  drawings, 99
  frame-and-panel door, 105
  frame/case assembly, 102–04
  notching top, 101
  three-part back, 103, 104
Cabinet cases, plywood, 162–73
  about: overview of, 162
  bottom and back, 168–69
  core materials importance, 162–66
  corner inlay, 170, 173
  doweling jig, 170
  drawings, 165, 171
  final assembly, 172
  frame-and-panel case, 163, 165, 166

front, 170
  gluing in splines, 167
  legs, 167–68
  mitered cases, 163, 166–72
  options and possibilities, 163
  perfect alignment, 169
  side panels, 167, 169
  stiles, 170
  tenon mortises, 167–68
  veneering substrate, 164
Cabinets. *See also* Country hutch, making; *Kitchen island references*
  appliance garage sliding door, 96, 97
  backsplashes and, 95, 136, 144
  beautiful plywood cases. *See* Cabinet cases, plywood
  bowfront. *See* Cabinet, bowfront wall
  cabinetmaker's galley kitchen, 93–97
  categories of, 120 (*see also* Cabinets, semicustom)
  clever solutions, 95
  new approach to. *See* Cabinets, classic, new approach to
  roll-out shelf with stainless appliance panel, 96, 97
  semicustom. *See* Cabinets, installing semicustom; Cabinets, semicustom
  Shaker hanging. *See* Cabinet, simple hanging
  sliding gate with, 96, 97
  vanity. *See Bathroom vanity references*
Cabinets, classic, new approach to, 205–13
  about: overview of, 205
  assembly and alignment, 208
  doors and butt hinges, 207, 210, 213
  face frame construction, 206, 207, 208
  joinery, 210–12
  modernizing the style, 205–07
  process, illustrated, 206–13
  scribing for tight fit, 209

starting with right materials, 207
Cabinets, installing semicustom, 132–41
  about: overview of, 132
  clamping cabinets to join, 138
  corner cabinets first, 135, 136
  establishing reference line, 134
  first cabinet to install, 135, 136
  joining cabinets, 135, 138
  measuring/marking for level, 132–34
  organizing space for, 133
  plumbing/electrical connections and, 138, 139
  pre-installation steps, 132–34
  scribing end panels, 140, 141
  setting cabinets, 135–41
  shimming tips and tricks, 135, 137
  trim installation tips, 140–41
  unpacking cabinets, 132, 133, 134
  upper cabinets, 136, 137–38
Cabinets, semicustom, 120–31
  about: overview of, 120
  assessing quality, 127–29
  box quality, 127, 128
  Canyon Creek®, 120, 121, 122, 123, 127, 129, 131
  characteristics and options, 120–23
  cost considerations (options, upgrades, etc.), 124–26
  custom cabinets compared to, 131
  door quality, 127–29
  doors and shelves, 123
  drawer quality, 127, 128
  face-frames or frameless, 122–23
  finish choices/quality, 128, 129
  hardware and, 124

If you like this book, you'll love *Fine Homebuilding*.

Read *Fine Homebuilding* Magazine:

Get eight issues, including our two annual design issues, *Houses* and *Kitchens & Baths*, plus FREE tablet editions. Packed with expert advice and skill-building techniques, every issue provides the latest information on quality building and remodeling.

Subscribe today at:
FineHomebuilding.com/4Sub

Discover our *Fine Homebuilding* Online Store:

It's your destination for premium resources from America's best builders: how-to and design books, DVDs, videos, special interest publications, and more.

Visit today at:
FineHomebuilding.com/4More

Get our FREE *Fine Homebuilding* eNewsletter:

Keep up with the current best practices, the newest tools, and the latest materials, plus free tips and advice from *Fine Homebuilding* editors.

Sign up, it's free:
FineHomebuilding.com/4Newsletter

Become a FineHomebuilding.com member:

Join to enjoy unlimited access to premium content and exclusive benefits, including: 1,400+ articles; 350 tip, tool, and technique videos; our how-to video project series; over 1,600 field-tested tips; monthly giveaways; tablet editions; contests; special offers; and more.

Discover more information online:
FineHomebuilding.com/4Join

© 2018 The Taunton Press